THE PILGRIM COOKBOOK
RECIPES FROM GERMAN CHURCH LADIES

REPRINTED AND REVISED
BY NEW YORK HISTORY REVIEW

The Pilgrim Cookbook - Recipes from German Church Ladies

Copyright ©2019 New York History Review. Some rights reserved.

First published by The Ladies' Aid Society of Pilgrim Evangelical Lutheran Church, Chicago, Illinois in 1921 - reprinted and revised by New York History Review in 2019

ISBN: 978-1-950822-00-3
Printed in the United States of America

Cover image: Wiener Schnitzel, recipe page 44.

Good cooks are born, not made,
they say.
The saying's most untrue.
Hard trying and prime recipes
Will make good cooks of you.

From the publisher

All of my relatives "came over" from Germany to the United States starting in the 1830s and ending when my mom got off the boat in 1957. Half went to Illinois and half to New York. When the women arrived they found that cooking was not the same.

The ingredients were different, hard to find, or nonexistent. Stoves and ovens had different temperatures. Butcher shops, bakeries, and general goods like back home were blended into supermarkets here.

How did they cope? My female relatives banded together with other German church ladies and figured out how to do the best that they could do in this new land. They shared their secrets and shortcuts with each other. They kept their heritage alive in a new place.

-Diane Janowski

TABLE OF CONTENTS

Soups..9
Fish...15
Meats...23
"One Piece" Luncheons......................................45
Vegetables..55
Salads...67
Puddings and Desserts......................................89
Gelatine Desserts...105
Pies...111
Cheese and Eggs..119
Dumplings and Noodles.................................125
Fritters, Doughnuts, and Pancakes.................131
Baking Powder Breads and Coffee Cakes.....137
Yeast Breads..145
Cookies..153
Small Cakes...165
Icings and Fillings...169
Cakes..175
Torten...207
Ice Cream and Beverages................................215
Jams..219
Canned Fruits and Vegetables........................225
Ketchups, Pickles, Etc....................................228
Candies...239
Miscellaneous..244
Index...249

The original Pilgrim Evangelical Lutheran Church, Chicago, Illinois in 1921. Now known as Pilgrim Lutheran Church, relocated in the 1952 to 4300 North Winchester Avenue.

SOUPS

Cream of Green Bean Soup

Cook cut beans and 2 good-sized potatoes till tender; strain, saving water. Take out potatoes and mash them. Brown 1 tablespoon butter and 1 tablespoon lard, add a little flour, the water in which beans were cooked, potatoes, beans and 1 cup cream.
— Mrs. A. Piepho.

Beef Soup

Take about 1 ½ pounds lean chuck and 1 pound smoked butt, cover with water and boil about two hours. Then add 2 large carrots diced, 1 large German celery root or celeriac, 1 large German parsley root, 1 large stalk leek, and boil 1 hour more; salt to taste. Boil dried peas separately, flavor with sweet marjoram and add to soup just before serving. Navy beans may be used if preferred, or dumplings are also very good.
— Mrs. W. H. Jacobs.

Beer Soup

Pour 1 pint water in a kettle and set over fire. When hot add 1 pint beer, a little salt, ½ cup sugar, 1 quart milk, a little flour to thicken and 3 to 4 egg yolks. Serve with toasted bread squares,

and on top put the beaten egg whites to which has been added a little sugar and vanilla.
— Mrs. H. G. Tischer.

Cherry Soup

One pint canned cherries, 1 quart water, little stick cinnamon, 1 tablespoon farina. Put in some dumplings. Sweeten to taste. — Mrs. A. Steging.

Cherry Soup

One quart fresh cherries, 1 quart water, ¼ cup sugar, 1 broken stick cinnamon, ½ lemon sliced fine, 2 tablespoons tapioca, 1 egg yolk. Cook tapioca in 1 cup of boiling water until clear, add more water as it evaporates. Put in the first six ingredients and let boil 15 minutes. Take from fire, add carefully the well beaten yolk mixed with a little water. Froth beaten dry with a little sugar on top.
— Mrs. O. Kleppisch.

Cream of Clam Soup

Wash the clams, put them into a pan, pour boiling water over them and cover them tight. Let stand for about ten or fifteen minutes. Then take them out and remove black heads, flour them and season with a little nutmeg, mace, pepper and salt. Take three quarts of the liquid and put it into a saucepan to boil. To ½ pound of butter rub well 3 tablespoons of flour

and stir it into the liquid. Put in the clams and let them boil fifteen minutes. If you wish, add 1 pint of cream or milk.
—Mrs. R. Albrecht.

Corn Chowder

One can corn
1 large onion
4 cups potatoes
4 cups scalded milk
1 ½ inch cube salt pork,
8 crackers
1 or 2 stalks celery,
a part of a red or green
pepper, salt and a dash of paprika or cayenne pepper
4 cups boiling water

Cut the pork into small pieces, add onion and cook till light yellow, then add corn, 4 cups boiling water, onion and pork, and cook slowly 20 minutes with celery and pepper. Add potatoes cut in cubes and when done, add milk.
— Mrs. D. Wagner.

Corn Soup

Take ½ can corn and stew it with a slice of onion. Add salt and pepper to taste, and 1 quart of slightly thickened milk. Simmer for a minute, strain and serve. A few kernels of large popped corn are pretty floating on top of this soup.
— Alicia K. Steinhoff.

Milk Soup

Boil barley or rice in water until done, add a pinch of salt, sugar to taste, 1 or 2 pieces of stick cinnamon, a little butter and milk.
— Mrs. Semmlow.

Fresh Mushroom Soup

In 6 cups of water boil 1 large onion, tops of some celery, ½ green pepper for 30 minutes. Let stand 30 minutes then strain. In 2 ½ tablespoons butter simmer 1 cup of fresh sliced mushrooms for 10 minutes, add 2 ½ tablespoons flour and stock; simmer 15 minutes. When of right consistency add ¾ cup cream. Add 1 tablespoon whipped cream when serving; add salt and pepper to taste.
— Ada Wilson Bohnsack.

Green Pea Soup

Take 1 can peas, add 6 to 8 cups water, ½ cup carrots, diced, a little celery, 1 teaspoon salt, 1 scant tablespoon sugar, a little white pepper, 2 large tablespoons chopped onions. Let this simmer until carrots are done, then cream 2 tablespoons butter with 1 large tablespoon flour and add to the soup.

Dumplings for soup: 1 tablespoon butter, creamed, ½ teaspoon salt, 1 egg yolk, 1 cup milk, the beaten white of 1 egg and enough flour to thicken. Drop by spoonful into soup and boil about 15 minutes. — Mrs. H. G. Tischer.

Potato Soup

Four large potatoes, 1 small onion in which 6 cloves have been stuck, piece of celery or celery salt; cook until potatoes fall to pieces; take out onion and celery and mash the potatoes fine, pour in boiling milk until consistency of thick cream; beat one egg and take tablespoonful of butter and some canned corn into this. Season with salt.
— Mrs. A. Steging.

Cream of Potato Soup

Three potatoes
1 quart milk
1 teaspoon chopped parsley
3 teaspoons butter
1 teaspoon salt
½ teaspoon pepper
2 slices onion
2 teaspoons flour

Cook potatoes until tender, drain and rub through sieve. Scald milk and onion (simmer onion), add the butter and flour which have been blended together; add potatoes and cook 10 minutes.
— Mrs. Sodeman.

Cream of Tomato Soup

Press enough cooked tomatoes through a fine sieve to make 1 ½ cups; let puree become very hot. Melt ¼ cup butter, cook

in it ¼ cup flour, dash of pepper, and 1 scant teaspoon salt. When the mixture is frothy gradually stir in 1½ cups cream diluted with ½ cup water. Stir and cook until the sauce boils vigorously, then add the hot tomato puree and remove from fire at once.
— Olga T. Bohnsack.

Turnip Soup

Wash, pare and cut into small pieces 6 medium-sized white turnips. Boil them in unsalted water until tender, then rub through a fine sieve. Chop fine 1 small onion, put in a stew pan with 1 tablespoon butter, and cook slowly without browning for five minutes; then add 1 tablespoon flour and when blended, 1 quart of milk. Stir until boiling hot, add the turnip pulp and season well with salt and pepper. Cook slowly for 5 minutes; serve at once and pass grated cheese with it.
— Mrs. Albrecht.

Wine Soup

Boil ½ cup fine pearl tapioca in about 1 quart water until clear; then add a small piece of stick cinnamon, a little salt, 1 large glass wine (white or red), and finally 2 to 3 egg yolks and 2 to 3 tablespoons sugar. Serve also with toasted white bread squares and drop the beaten egg whites in little mounds
on top.
— Mrs. H. G. Tischer.

FISH

OYSTER COCKTAIL

Open 6 or more small oysters into a cup or glass that has been generously buried in ice, taking care to save the liquor. Season with salt and pepper and add 1 tablespoon of tomato ketchup, a few drops of lemon juice, a drop of Tabasco sauce and a dash of Worcestershire sauce.
— Johanna Kretschmer.

ANGELS ON HORSEBACK

Select large plump oysters and a corresponding number of very thin slices of boneless bacon. Pick over, wash and dry the oysters, and season them with black pepper. Wrap each in a slice of bacon and pin with a wooden toothpick; the round orange wood variety is best for this purpose. Place a frying pan over the fire, and when hot drop in sufficient prepared oysters to cover the bottom of the pan. Turn them quickly several times until the bacon is lightly browned, then serve at once on a hot platter.
— Mrs. R. Albrecht.

Oysters in Grapefruit Shells

Take all the pulp from halves of grapefruit and fill the shell with chipped ice. Make five depressions in the ice and lay an oyster in each with a lemon quarter in the center. Pass horseradish or cocktail dressing and thin strips of buttered brown bread; use grape fruit pulp for salad or for fruit cup.
— Alicia K. Steinhoff.

Escalloped Oysters

Examine oysters carefully and remove all pieces of shells. Then to 1 quart oysters and to 1 quart cracker crumbs add 1½ pints milk, salt and pepper, and a little melted butter. Stir all together and bake 1 hour.
— Mrs. M. Brockman.

Creole Crabs

One can crab meat
2 tablespoons butter
2 tablespoons chopped onion
2 tablespoons flour
2 cups tomato
¼ teaspoon salt
⅛ teaspoon pepper
few grains red pepper

Melt butter, add onion and cook slowly until yellow; add flour; when smooth, add tomatoes. Cook 10 minutes, then add sea-

sonings and crab meat. Serve on slices of hot buttered toast and garnish with strips of pimientos.
— Alicia K. Steinhofif.

Creamed Shrimps and Peas

One-half pint milk, piece of butter size of an egg. Heat in frying pan, salt to taste and thicken with corn starch. Remove from fire, add 1 can shrimps and ½ can peas. This is a nice dish for supper.
— Mrs. O. A. Skibbe.

Codfish Balls

Soak codfish (cut in pieces) about 1 hour in lukewarm water; remove skin and bones, shred, and put on stove in cold water. As soon as water begins to boil, pour it off, add fresh cold water and bring to a boil again. Have ready potatoes boiled tender, mashed and seasoned with butter. Take twice as much potato as codfish and while both are still warm form into balls. Fry in deep, hot lard, or drippings, like doughnuts. An egg makes them lighter. If cold potatoes are used reheat them with a little cream and butter.
— Mrs. H. G. Tischer.

Baked Fish with Tomatoes

Clean well, sprinkle with salt 1 hour before cooking, rub flour over it and baste with butter and put in baking pan; pour a can of tomatoes over fish and season well with salt and pepper and bake.
— Mrs. Albrecht.

BAKED FISH

Clean thoroughly, sprinkle with salt an hour before cooking, fill with dressing and sew securely, sprinkle flour over it, baste with butter and place in dripping pan in moderate oven; allow 1½ hours for a good sized fish; serve with drawn butter sauce and garnish with sliced lemon.
— Mrs. Albrecht.

BAKED CREAM FISH

You may use salmon, Finnan Haddie, lobster, or any left-over cooked fish. Make a white sauce of 2 tablespoons butter, 2 tablespoons flour, and 1 cup milk. Mix fish with sauce adding salt, pepper, paprika, chopped green pepper, strips of pimiento, and a little chopped onion, as desired. Place in a buttered baking dish or in ramekins, spread bread crumbs over top and bake until brown.
— Alicia K. Steinhoff.

FRIED FISH WITH STUFFING

Any small fish may be used. Scale, clean and open the fish down the belly. Have ready an onion cut in slender strips, some tiny red peppers with the seeds removed, and some fresh mint leaves. Place in each fish a strip of onion, a pepper, and a mint leaf. Skewer the fish closely together with a wooden toothpick, roll in flour, season with salt and a very little

cayenne, and fry in hot lard or butter. Fry until a crisp brown and serve with a garnish of mint leaves.
— Mrs. R. Albrecht.

Halibut with Sauce

Brush a slice of halibut with melted butter, sprinkle with salt and pepper, cover with a paper and bake 15 minutes. Serve with Hollandaise sauce made with ¾ cup butter, 2 egg yolks, and ⅛ tablespoon vinegar.
— Mrs. G. C. Hass.

Boiled Fish with Green Sauce

Enough water to cover fish, 3 or 4 bay leaves, 18 peppercorns, 1 onion, salt and ½ cup vinegar. Bring all to a boil, then put in the fish and cook slowly until tender, about 15 to 20 minutes. Place fish on a warm platter and pour over it a

Green Sauce.
— Melt 2 tablespoons butter in a pan, add 1 tablespoon flour and cook until a light brown color; then add enough of the water in which the fish was boiled to make a creamy sauce. Remove from fire and add the juice of ½ lemon, 1 cup of finely chopped parsley and 1 or 2 egg yolks.
— Alicia K. Steinhoff.

Salmon Balls

One can of salmon, 12 rolled soda crackers, 1 cup milk, salt, 2 eggs. Form into balls and fry a light brown.
— Mrs. Sodeman.

Boiled Salmon

Take 2 or 4 pounds of salmon, scrape the skin, wipe, tie in cheesecloth and immerse in gently boiling water. Cover and cook from 20 to 40 minutes or until the fish will leave the bone easily. Drain and remove the skin. Arrange on platter and pour egg or white sauce over and around. Garnish with hard boiled eggs and lemon points and serve with cucumbers and potato balls.
— Mrs. E. S. Berndt.

Salmon Loaf

One can salmon, 1 cup milk, ½ cup ground bread or crackers, 1 egg, salt and pepper to taste. Bake 1 hour. May be served with tomato sauce.
— Mrs. H. England.

Baked Trout

Scale trout and remove head. Season and stuff with a dressing made of bread crumbs and onions to which has been added a pinch of salt, 1 egg and a lump of butter. Place in oblong baking dish and cover with canned tomatoes.

Bake in a moderate oven 30 minutes. Just before removing from oven, add a little flour and water or milk to make a cream gravy with the tomato sauce. Dot fish with small pieces of butter before placing in oven.
— Clara L. Kemnitz.

Boiled Trout with Cream Sauce

Boil a 3-pound trout; skin and pick out all bones. Put on a hot platter and pour over it a cream sauce made of 1 pint milk, 2 tablespoons butter, 1 tablespoon flour, 2 eggs, a pinch of salt and parsley cut up fine.
— Mrs. Sodeman.

Baked White Fish

Clean, open, and straighten the fish out. Take backbone out, beginning at the head and remove carefully. All the other bones will come out with it. Salt and allow to stand some time. Dredge the fish well with cracker crumbs and lay in a pan, skin side down. Lay bits of drippings over the top and it will brown fine. Ordinary fish will bake in 15 to 20 minutes.
— Mrs. H. Stiede.

Emanuel German Evangelical Church, 324 West Main Street, Manchester, Michigan. The church is on the list of Michigan State Historical Sites.

MEATS

STUFFING FOR TURKEY OR GOOSE

Soak 2 loaves of stale bread, 2 teaspoons salt, ½ teaspoon pepper, 2 teaspoons minced parsley, 2 teaspoons or more of sage, 1 egg. Boil heart, liver and gizzard until tender and put through food chopper with 2 medium sized onions and brown mixture in butter. Mix all well — fill fowl and sew up. One-half pound of chopped meat may be added if more meat is desired.
— Elise Rauschert.

PEANUT DRESSING

Three-quarters cup cracker crumbs, ½ cup shelled peanuts, finely chopped, ½ cup heavy cream, 2 tablespoons melted butter, a few drops onion juice, salt and pepper to taste. Mix in order given. Very good with roast duck.
— Mrs. Wm. Fredericks.

CRANBERRY SAUCE

One quart cranberries, 2 tart apples. Cover with cold water and boil together until soft. While hot rub through a sieve and return to fire, adding 1 cup granulated sugar to 2 cups sauce. Boil up and remove from fire. Serve cold.
— Mrs. C. B. Moellering.

SPICED CRANBERRY SAUCE

Three cups cranberries, 1 cup water, 2 cups sugar, 2 teaspoons vinegar, 1 teaspoon each of cloves and cinnamon. Place cranberries with the water in a granite pan and cook slowly until soft. Add the sugar, vinegar and spices to the cranberries and let boil another ten minutes. Pour into dish to cool.

HORSERADISH SAUCE

Have 1 cup of thick cream, thoroughly chilled, and whip it with an egg-beater till very stiff. It should keep its shape. Add ½ teaspoon salt, ¼ teaspoon pepper, 3 tablespoons grated horseradish. The radish should be fresh, if possible, add 2 tablespoons vinegar and 1 teaspoon sugar, put in ice-box until ready to use, as it should be very thick when served. Good with veal chops.
— Mrs. H. G. Tischer.

SAVORY PUDDING

To be eaten with hot meats. Take 4 tablespoons of flour, 1 or 2 eggs; beat well, add milk until about as thick as a pancake batter, then add 1 small chopped onion, 2 tablespoons oatmeal, a little sage, pepper, salt, and about 1½ tablespoons chopped suet, or butter. Pour into pan containing very hot fat and bake about 30 minutes in a rather hot oven. Very savoury just served with gravy.
— Mrs. F. Ingham.

CREAMED CHICKEN

Boil chicken until tender as for soup, with celery and parsley. When tender dice the breast of chicken. Parboil one pair sweetbreads and dice also. Pour hot water over small can of mushrooms and let drain in colander, quarter mushrooms and add to chicken and sweetbreads.

SAUCE

1 cup chicken broth thickened with 1 tablespoon flour and 1 tablespoon butter creamed together; add a little pepper. Put chicken, sweetbreads and mushrooms into sauce, lastly add i cup stiffly whipped cream. Put in ramekins and grate a very few crumbs over top. Stand ramekins in pan containing warm water and brown under broiler or oven.
— Johanna Kretchmer.

CREAMED CHICKEN ON TOAST

One large chicken, 2 cans mushrooms, 2 large green peppers, 4 medium stalks celery. Cook the chicken until tender, remove bones and cut in small pieces. Add celery, peppers, mushrooms, and 4 cups of stock. Thicken with flour and add 2 bottles of cream. Season to taste. Serve on toasted white bread.
— Mrs. H. Trippler.

Chicken Loaf

Cut up chicken and boil until tender, remove bones and put meat through the chopper. Add 1 cup of ground stale bread crumbs, 1 egg, salt and pepper; mix well, form into a loaf and bake 45 minutes. Chop giblets, add to chicken broth and thicken a little. When loaf is ready to serve, pour gravy over and around it.

This loaf sliced cold with the addition of thinly sliced onions makes an excellent filling for sandwiches of either white or brown bread.
— Mrs. E. S. Berndt.

Boston Baked Chicken

Cut a chicken into small pieces as for stewing, wash and wipe dry; sprinkle with salt and dip each piece in melted butter, then coat with flour. Put into a bean pot, laying the larger pieces in the bottom of pot and putting any pieces of chicken fat on top. Pour over the chicken 1½ cups boiling water and cover tightly with the lid. If the chicken is a young one bake 90 minutes. The juices, fat and flour will make an excellent gravy. Take out chicken when done and arrange with the gravy on a dish or serve direct from the bean pot, first seasoning to taste.
— Josephine O'Rourke.

Chicken Smothered in Sauerkraut

Procure a young chicken, rub well with a flour and water paste; wipe quite dry inside, dust with salt and pepper. Rinse and drain 1 quart sauerkraut, fill chicken with hot mashed potatoes well-seasoned, lay it in the roaster and place on it two slices of bacon (place two slices in bottom of roaster also), then cover the chicken completely with sauerkraut, add a ¼ teaspoon of salt and half that quantity of pepper. Pour over a cup of cold water. Close down the lid tight and roast in the oven 3 hours; have a moderate fire.

Do not allow to cook dry; add boiling water as required to keep bottom of roaster quite moist. When done lift chicken on to a large platter, pile the kraut around it and garnish with slices of lemon. To the sauce in roaster add a large tablespoon of browned flour and a cup of stock; boil up, add salt and pepper to taste. Strain and serve in sauce tureen.
— Mrs. E. S. Berndt.

Chicken Turkish Style

One chicken weighing about 4 pounds, 2 cups rice, 3 cups broth, 1 bunch soup greens. Cut chicken in pieces, put on to boil in salted water with soup greens. When nearly tender take out and place a layer of chicken in a pan, then a layer of rice and continue until all is used. Add 3 cups broth to each cup of rice, put on back of stove, cover tight and do not open until wanted.
— Mrs. Roth.

Meat or Chicken Pie

Make a dough as for baking powder biscuits. Have meat or chicken boiled tender. Line bake pan with dough to within an inch from the bottom, lay meats or chicken in, add some gravy, butter, salt and pepper. Cover with crust of dough, and bake about 30 minutes.
— Mrs. Edw. J. Keuer.

Chicken Shortcake

Make a good shortcake, when baked split it open and spread it with a liberal layer of hot fricasseed chicken from which the bones have been removed. Place the other half of the shortcake on top and pour over it a liberal amount of the chicken gravy. Serve upon a deep platter or in a big vegetable dish. The shortcake should be well moistened with the gravy.
— Mrs. E. S. Berndt.

Chicken a La King

Heat 2 tablespoons butter, add 1 green pepper chopped fine; cook slowly 3 minutes, add 1 tablespoon flour, rich cream enough to make sauce and 2 cups chopped chicken. Heat thoroughly.
— Helen Lindau.

Duck and Rice

Select a fat duck, cut it in neat pieces and put to boil with 2 quarts water, 1 onion sliced thin, 3 sliced tomatoes, a bit of garlic, 1 yellow pepper chopped fine, and salt to taste. When about half done add 1 cup rice and let boil as nearly dry as possible. Very good.
— Mrs. Albrecht.

Ducklings, Indian Style

Chop very fine 2 onions and 1 clove of garlic and fry slowly in 2 tablespoons of butter until brown; add 1 tablespoon of curry powder and 2 minutes later 1 pound of raw lean beef chopped fine. Draw to one side of fire and cook slowly for 15 minutes, stirring well. Let cool and stuff 2 ducks which have been cleaned and wiped. Fasten into shape, for roasting brush them over with chutney sauce and put in a hot oven. In 15 minutes begin to baste, repeating the basting every 10 minutes. Roast for | of an hour and serve with gravy, garnishing with watercress and slices of lemon.
— Mrs. R. Albrecht.

Roast Rabbit

Skin, clean, and let rabbit lie in cold water for about 3 hours; then take out and dry. Put rabbit in baking pan, pour over it ¼ pound butter, which has been melted and browned, and roast in a real hot oven for 15 minutes. Then add 1 cup sour cream and roast for 20 minutes. Take out, thicken gravy and serve.
— Mrs. A. Piepho.

Steamed Rabbit

Brown 1 onion in butter, add the rabbit cut in pieces and cook until brown. Then add a few slices of bacon, salt and pepper, a little cayenne, parsley and celery seed. Thicken with flour and add 1 cup cream. Very good.
— Mrs. H. G. Tischer.

Hasenpfeffer

After cleaning and washing rabbits well, cut in pieces and cover with vinegar to which add 2 bay leaves, 12 whole cloves, allspice, 24 whole peppers. Let stand for 2 hours, then take out meat and dry, turn in flour and fry brown in ½ pound butter and bacon. Salt it, then put back into vinegar and simmer for 1½ hours, adding water occasionally as needed. Just before meat is done add about 6 ginger snaps; this flavors the gravy nicely.
— Mrs. A. Streger.

Hasenpfeffer

Skin the rabbit, then cut into small pieces and put into weak vinegar or buttermilk with whole onions, whole black pepper, bay leaves, cloves, allspice and sliced lemons. Let stand for 24 hours and then strain off. Place the rabbit in a pan with butter and chopped onions and roast it slowly in the oven. Before it is done add browned butter and flour. Bake until tender and season with the strained off vinegar.
— Mrs. Chas. Hemler.

French Chopped Beef

Take one pound chopped round steak, little pork, add pepper and salt, 1 egg, little bread which has been softened in water, fry in butter; stir frequently so it will not get hard.
— Mrs, Louise M. Lafrentz.

Beef Loaf

Three pounds beef
½ pound raw ham
3 eggs well beaten
3 soda crackers rolled fine
1 teaspoon salt
1 teaspoon pepper,
3 tablespoons cream
6 hard boiled eggs

Chop the beef and ham very fine and then add the salt and pepper, the cracker crumbs, the well beaten eggs and the cream. Mix all these together perfectly, grease a baking pan thoroughly and press half the mixture into it firmly. Trim each end of your hard boiled eggs so as to make a flat surface, then put them on top of the mixture in the loaf pan, placing them in a row, end to end. Now pack on top the balance of the meat, pressing it down firmly. Cover and bake in a moderate oven 1 hour. Uncover and bake half an hour longer. Serve either hot or cold in slices.
— Mrs. Lachmann.

Beef Tenderloin

Wipe clean, but do not wash the tenderloin; season with salt and pepper. Place in roasting pan, adding a little water, 1 large onion, 1 carrot; roast in lower oven of gas range until brown and crisp. Place in upper oven, add the mushrooms, which have been prepared, and roast 15 minutes longer. Roast meat 15 minutes to the pound.

Mushroom Sauce. Boil dry mushrooms in salt water 1 hour. Prepare a sauce of 1 tablespoon butter, 1 small onion cut in very small pieces and 1 tablespoon flour. Add this to mushrooms, do not drain water, pour this over roast.
— Miss L. Gansz.

Flank Steak

Brown on both sides in butter, to keep juice in steak, salt and pepper, then turn over a can of tomatoes with sauce and bake 1½ hours in self-basting pan.
— Mrs. O. Kleppisch.

Pot Roast with Carrots

Make a pot roast as usual. In a separate kettle put 2 bunches of carrots scraped and cut in small pieces, 1 tablespoon butter, 2 tablespoons sugar, pinch of salt; cover with water and simmer until water has boiled off, then add gravy from the pot roast a little at a time, using just enough to keep carrots from burning.

Stir often. When done there should not be much gravy on the carrots, but just nice and moist. Will take about 3 hours.
— Mrs. A. Piepho.

German Sauerbraten

Put 3 or 4 pounds of beef shoulder in vinegar for 2 or 3 days; add an onion, bay leaf and whole pepper seeds. When ready to use put lard in kettle and brown meat a nice brown, then add a little water and some of the vinegar; it must not be too sour. Let simmer until tender then add a few ginger snaps and browned flour to thicken.
— Mrs. C. Sommer.

Swiss Steak

Take a thick round steak from 2 to 2½ inches in thickness and pound into it as much flour as it will take, using the edge of a plate. When the flour has been pounded into both sides take the meat and brown it on both sides; remove to a sauce pan. Heat ½ can tomatoes, 1 large onion cut fine, 1 sweet pepper, and pour over meat. Cover tightly and cook slowly for 2 to 3 hours. Just before meat is done season to taste. Delicious when served hot, also nice cold.
— Josephine O'Rourke.

Baked Swiss Steak

Take about 1¼ pounds of round steak and pound in as much flour as it will hold. Heat lard and bacon drippings in a frying pan, add steak, salt and pepper and a little onion, if liked. Brown meat on both sides, then add enough water to nearly fill the pan, and place pan and all in the oven. Bake slowly 1 hour, or until tender.
— Mrs. C. Feig.

Swiss Steak with Peas

Get a round steak about 1 inch thick. Knead in as much flour as it will hold, fry in butter, add sliced onion and season to taste. Then pour over it 1 can of peas and let simmer about 10 minutes.
— Olga T. Bohnsack.

Sour Beef Tongue

Boil tongue the day before wishing to serve. When done, skin, then put back into liquid until ready to make the following gravy: 2 cups of the liquid, 2 tablespoons butter, 1 tablespoon flour, 8 ginger snaps, lemon or vinegar to taste, ½ cup claret wine, sugar to taste, ½ package raisins, 1 bay leaf. Slice tongue, pour gravy over it and serve.
— Mrs. W. C. Pfister.

Beef Tongue with Vegetables

Boil a salted beef tongue until almost tender. Remove skin and all fat, and allow to stand in liquid. In 2 good sized tablespoons butter, brown 2 carrots, 1 onion, 1 large potato, 1 turnip, all cut into pieces; add a bay leaf, a few sprigs of parsley. Brown until tender, then add a quart of the stock, put the tongue in it, place in oven in a covered pan, and allow to roast 2 hours, turning the tongue once. After 2 hours, rub the vegetables through a colander, add a tablespoon flour, rubbed smooth with a cup of tomato juice, salt and pepper to taste, a little Worcestershire sauce. Allow all to boil up and serve on tongue, which has been cut into slices.
— Johanna Kretchmer.

Head Cheese

Two pounds pork shoulder, 2 pork shanks, 2 pounds veal; boil pork and veal separately until well done, then take out and when partly cool, cut into small pieces; strain the water in which both the veal and pork was boiled, add it to the meat; flavor with onion, pepper and salt, and if it is liked sour, add vinegar to suit taste; let it come to a good boil; set away to cool.
— Mrs. H. W. Bruedigam.

Sulze

Place in kettle 1 veal bone with meat, 1 small tongue, 1 small pork shank or pig's feet, 1½ cups vinegar, 2 large onions, 8 cloves, handful salt, a little pepper, and 3 bay leaves. Cover with water and cook for 2½ hours. Then take out meat, cut it off the bones

and dice it. Put equal parts of meat and stock (liquid in which meat was boiled) in deep bowls and set in a cool place until jellied.
— Mrs. A. Piepho.

BOILED SHOULDER OF MUTTON WITH OYSTERS

Trim and wipe a thick shoulder of mutton, bone it and dust lightly with pepper and mace. Over the inside of the meat spread two dozen good sized oysters, roll and tie tightly. Put in a saucepan with 1 onion, ½ teaspoon salt, and 1 small red pepper; cover with boiling water and simmer 15 minutes to the pound. Melt together 1 tablespoon butter and 2 scant tablespoons flour, add 1 pint of the meat liquor, stir until smooth and thick, seasoning with salt and pepper. Then add 1 teaspoon lemon juice, 1 teaspoon finely chopped parsley, 12 oysters, and simmer until the edges of the oysters curl. Serve in gravy boat with the meat.
— Mrs. R. Albrecht.

GRITS

Cover 1 pound steel cut oats with hot water and boil slowly for 1 hour or more, stirring often and adding water if needed. When oats are well cooked but not watery, add 1 large tablespoon of salt or more, ½ teaspoon ground pepper, ½ teaspoon ground allspice, 1 tablespoon of sage, sweet marjoram and thyme mixed and mashed very fine, 1 small onion cut fine, the cracklings from one dollar's worth of leaf lard, and stir all well together, then put in a large bowl to cool. Cut in slices about ¾ inch thick and fry a nice brown. This is very good for breakfast in the winter.
— Mrs. W. H. Jacobs.

Country Style Sausage

One large onion, ½ pound steel cut oats, whole oats or barley may be used, ¾ pound pork from the shoulder, salt to flavor, 4 tablespoons or more of thyme to taste. Boil meat until done, then put it through meat chopper. Boil oatmeal in the water of the meat, add the chopped meat and thyme. Set in cool place, fry when served.
— Mrs. Semmlow.

Meat Loaf

Two pounds round steak, 1 pound lean fresh pork ground fine, 1 cup cooked tomatoes, 2 eggs, 1 cup cracker crumbs, salt to taste. Form into loaf, press hard into a paper-lined pan. Place several strips of bacon on top. Bake slowly for 30 minutes and rapidly for 15 minutes. Make gravy from liquid which exudes.
— Mrs. Theo. Doering.

Meatballs in Tomato Sauce

One pound chopped pork 1½ pounds chopped round steak, add ½ loaf stale bread soaked in water, then press out water. Mix well and season with salt, pepper, a little chopped onion, if liked, and 1 egg. Form into balls and drop into tomato sauce made as follows: Rub 1 quart can tomatoes through colander, put back in sauce pan, add 1 bay leaf and small onion. When it boils drop in the meat balls and cook 20 or 30 minutes. If gravy is too thin thicken it.
— Mrs. E. S. Berndt.

Meatballs

Mix together equal quantities of cooked and chopped veal and raw chopped beef. Add ⅓ as much soaked bread crumbs as you have meat. Season with salt and pepper and stir in a raw egg, beaten. Form with the hands into balls, set in the icebox to stiffen, roll in eggs and cracker crumbs, leave in the icebox for a half hour longer, then fry in deep fat.
— Mrs. A. Steging.

Sauerkraut

Place sauerkraut in an earthen or stone crock, with some of its juice and a good-sized piece of fresh pork or sausage, adding a little water if dry. Place a granite pie plate over it and set in the oven. Bake slowly for 2½ hours, removing the lid only to stir a few times.
— Mrs. E. S. Berndt.

Sweetbread Princess

Soak sweetbreads in warm water for 20 minutes and lift out in cold water for 15 minutes; drain and remove the gristle and skin. Parboil for a few minutes then cool. Salt, pepper and dredge with flour. Put a liberal quantity of butter in a frying pan, heat and put sweetbreads in this for 15 minutes and brown. Serve on artichoke bottoms.
— Mrs. E. S. Berndt.

Baked Spiced Ham

Soak the ham overnight in cold water. Next morning wash and scrape it well, then put in a large kettle, cover with cold water and bring slowly to a boil. Add 1 teaspoon each of whole cloves and peppercorns tied in thin muslin and, unless the ham is a very small one, simmer slowly for 2 hours. Take from the water and pull off the skin. Put in a pan in a moderate oven and bake for 2 hours, basting frequently; use a cup of sherry, a little at a time until it is all used, then baste with the drippings in the pan. Fifteen minutes before taking from the oven sprinkle thickly with brown sugar and let brown. Serve hot or cold.
— Mrs. R. Albrecht.

Escalloped Ham and Eggs

One pint white sauce, 6 hard-boiled eggs chopped, ½ pound boiled ham chopped, salt and pepper. To make the white sauce melt 2 tablespoons butter, add 2 tablespoons flour, and then a pint of milk; boil for a few minutes. In a buttered baking dish or casserole place a layer of ham, then a layer of eggs, then a layer of white sauce. Continue until dish is filled. Sprinkle top with bread crumbs and bits of butter. Bake in oven until top is browned.
— Alicia K. Steinhoff.

Boiled Pork with Cabbage

To a piece of lean pork shoulder or butt add water so it is nearly covered. Cut a cabbage into quarters and put with the meat. Add salt and pepper, a pinch of caraway seed and a pinch of sugar, if liked. Boil about 1½ to 2 hours.
— Mrs. W. H. Jacobs.

Breaded Pork Chops

Trim the chops neatly and wipe with a damp cloth. Dip in beaten egg, then in cracker meal and fry in deep fat. They are improved by the addition of tomato sauce.
— Mrs. E. S. Berndt.

Pork and Navy Beans

Any kind of pork will do spareribs are nice and as many beans as wanted. Clean beans, cook for about ½ hour, then add 1 teaspoon baking soda; let boil a few minutes and pour off water. Brown meat on all sides in frying pan, add 1 onion, beans and as much water as needed. Season. Boil until tender, adding water as needed. Beans do not have to be soaked if put on with cold water.
— Mrs. G. Lemar.

Pork Tenderloin Larded

Make a deep pocket lengthwise in each tenderloin and fill with a dressing made of 1 cup cracker crumbs, 2 tablespoons butter,

melted, seasoning and water enough to moisten, sew up pockets closely and cover tenderloin with strips of fat pork. Bake in a brisk oven 45 minutes, basting constantly with a brown sauce — 2 tablespoons butter, 2 tablespoons flour, ½ teaspoon salt, ¼ teaspoon pepper, 1 small onion, 1½ cups boiling water, 1/2 bay leaf. Cook onion in the butter until well browned, then remove it, add flour, seasonings and boiling water. Keep hot and baste tenderloins frequently.
— Mrs. G. C. Hass.

Mock Turkey

Two cups whole wheat bread crumbs, 2 cups ground walnuts, 2 eggs well beaten, 1 pint milk, 3 tablespoons butter, 1 tablespoon corn oil, pinch salt. Put together in the order given. Form into a loaf and bake 30 minutes; baste with butter and a little water.
— Mrs. O. Braun.

Mock Turkey

Take 2 fitting spare rib pieces, and fill with prunes (soaked in water), small pieces of apples, a handful of bread crumbs, sugar and a little cinnamon, and a small piece of butter. Salt the meat, place filling between the meat and sew together. Put into a pan with water and bake 2 hours in self-basting pan.
— Mrs. O. Kleppisch.

Filled Spare Ribs

Buy 2 large sides of spare ribs. Make a stuffing of diced apples, ½ package raisins, 2 eggs, bread crumbs, pepper, salt, cinnamon and a little sugar. Put stuffing between the ribs and bake in oven. Herbs may also be added to filling. This is a good substitute for turkey.
— Mrs. W. H. Jacobs.

Veal Croquettes

One cup cooked veal chopped fine, 1 tablespoon butter and 1 tablespoon flour mixed cold, a little salt, pepper, parsley, onion chopped; then pour ½ cup hot milk over all, stir smooth, add veal, stir and let cool. Roll balls in cracker crumbs and egg and fry in hot lard.
— Mrs. H. G. Tischer.

Veal Loaf

Two eggs, 1½ pounds chopped veal and pork a little celery or celery seed, ½ cup cracker crumbs, salt, pepper, and milk enough to moisten. Form in a loaf, bake, basting with tomato juice or sour cream.
— Miss L. Gansz.

Breast of Veal

Get a veal breast and have a pocket cut in. Take a stale white bread soak in water, drain water off. Beat 2 eggs light, add a little

browned butter, a little parsley, some grated nutmeg and salt to taste. Stir all together and fill into pocket; sew up the end of pocket. Baste with butter and put in oven.
— Mrs. C. Sommer.

Veal Cutlets with Tomato Sauce

Bread cutlets, and fry brown.
Tomato sauce: Fry, but do not brown, tablespoon fat, 1 tablespoon flour, 1 finely chopped onion, add 1 cup of tomato pulp, which has been carefully strained, cup water, 1 stalk finely chopped celery. Let boil a few minutes then season to taste.
— Mrs. Mandel Z.

Veal Sandwich

One slice raw ham, 2 large slices of veal from the leg, 1 onion, 1 bay leaf, about 1 cup sour milk. Make a sandwich by placing the ham between the veal slices. Place in a small roaster, adding the onion, bay leaf, and about 1 cup hot water. Bake in a medium oven until tender, then add the sour milk; bake about 10 minutes longer.

This is also very good when prepared with tomatoes, omitting the sour milk. Place meat in pan, add onion, bay leaf, ½ cup hot water and 1 can tomatoes. Bake until tender.
— Alicia K. Steinhoff.

Veal Collops

Take neat pieces of cold veal cut thin, dust them with a seasoning of nutmeg, mace, salt and cayenne, and sprinkle with a little lemon juice. Melt butter in a pan and fry veal slightly. Arrange on a hot dish. To the butter left in pan add 1 teaspoon Worcestershire sauce or ketchup, ½ teaspoon anchovy essence. Stir until thoroughly hot. Pour over veal, and serve with little rolls or fried bacon, fried bread and slices of lemon.
— Mrs. F. Ingham.

Veal Cutlets (Wiener Schnitzel)

2 pounds of veal cut into six ¾-inch pieces - pounded, salted and peppered. Beat 2 eggs, dip the meat into it, and then sprinkle with flour. Heat one stick of butter in pan and fry the meat on both sides. While frying, drip the juice of half a lemon on top. When done, place on hot platter. If desired, place a lightly fried egg on top of each.
-Mrs. Lina Meier

"One Piece" Luncheons

Boston Baked Beans

Soak 1 quart navy beans in cold water over night; boil in fresh water next morning. When they begin to soften, drain the water off and put beans in a bean pot or a gallon stone jar. Add 1 pound lean salt pork cut in pieces. 1 teaspoon dry mustard mixed with ½ cup good molasses, 1 small can tomatoes strained, and enough boiling water to cover beans. Add salt, if necessary, and more water also. Bake from 4 to 5 hours in slow oven.
— Mrs. Klipp.

Baked Beans with Ketchup

After soaking 1 quart of beans for a while put on to boil with 1 pound bacon cut in small pieces. Boil until hull begins to split, then pour into baking dish with all the liquor. Add 2 to 3 tablespoons sugar and 4 teaspoons mustard. Bake about 2 hours or until well done. Last of all add a 25-cent bottle of Heinz ketchup.
— Mrs. Albrecht.

Creamed Chipped Beef with Noodles

Two cups boiled noodles, 2 cups milk, 1 cup chipped beef, 1 tablespoon butter, 2 tablespoons flour. Mix flour and butter together, add milk, cook until creamy, then add the beef and lastly the noodles.
— Mrs. H. A. Zorn.

Chili Con Carne

One-half pound round steak cut into cubes, ½ pound pork cut in cubes, 1 carrot diced, 1 onion diced, 2 potatoes diced, 1 green pepper, 1 pinch red pepper. Simmer until tender; then add 1 can red kidney beans drained, 1 can tomato soup, 1 stalk celery. If liked, 3 slices of bacon, cut in cubes and fried brown, may be added with the bacon fat.
— Miss A. H. Rehm.

Chili Con Carne

Three-quarter pound beef, either shoulder or end of the round
1 No. 2 can of tomatoes
1½ cups of chili beans, or kidney beans.
Soup bone

Place soup bone in pot and cover with water; cook slowly like soup. Cut beef into very small pieces, fry until brown, add water and stew about an hour. Remove bone from soup, cut off meat if any and put back in the pot, add the stewed beef with the gravy, small piece of onion, salt, pepper, and the heated tomatoes. Put

the beans on to cook in a separate pot at the same time you cook the soup bone. Allow the beans to boil up, pour water off and add fresh water; cook till half done. Then stir beans into meat and tomato mixture, add red pepper to taste, and cook until beans are done.
— Mrs. Arthur Emde.

Chop Suey

Cut into small pieces 1 pound each of steak, veal shoulder, and pork shoulder. Brown a cup of onion in butter and add meat. When brown add 2 stalks celery, 1 can mushrooms, 1 tablespoon molasses, a little salt and 1 cup water. Let it stew over a slow fire 1½ hours, adding water as needed.
— Mrs. H. A. Zorn.

Chop Suey

Cut into small pieces 1 pound pork from the shoulder and 1 pound veal from the leg. Mix and fry slowly for 30 minutes. Then add 2 tablespoons molasses and small teaspoon salt. Fry 10 minutes more then add 2 cups onions cut into eighths, 2 cups celery cut into small pieces and fry all for 20 minutes. Sprinkle with flour several times during process. Add a little water, bring to a boil and serve with steamed rice.
— Mrs. P. Metzger.

Potato Loaf with Bacon and Peas

Rub a bread tin thoroughly with bacon drippings, then thickly as possible with dried bread crumbs. Pack in gently 1 quart of mashed potatoes and bake 30 minutes in quick oven. Unmold on platter, serve with a garnish on top of fried or broiled bacon and radish roses. Surround with peas.
— Mrs. A. J. Koehneke.

Sunday Evening Supper

Raw cabbage cut fine mixed with mayonnaise dressing. Form mountain on a large chop plate, place frankfurters around standing upward and sweet potato balls around the edge.
— Mrs. O. Kleppisch.

Stuffed Cabbage

Grind together 1 pound round steak and 1 cup bread crumbs and season with salt and pepper. Cut out the inside of a small head of cabbage and fill with the meat and bread crumbs, then tie it up in a napkin and boil for 2 hours. Take 4 potatoes, 1 onion, 1 carrot and cut in cubes; place these in the kettle with cabbage and meat, and boil until tender. Remove napkin and cut cabbage and meat in slices. Arrange vegetables around the meat and make a gravy of 1 cup milk, 1 cup stock seasoned with salt and pepper and parsley cut fine. Thicken with 1 tablespoon flour and pour over meat.
— Mrs. Chas. Hemler.

FILLED CABBAGE LEAVES

One medium head of cabbage, 1 cup rice, 1 small onion, 1½ pounds chopped meat. Soak rice for several hours in warm water. Season meat as for meat balls, and add rice. Separate cabbage and scald the leaves until they are soft. Place on each loaf some of the meat and rice mixture, then roll up leaf and pin together with toothpicks. Brown some flour in a pan, add water enough to make a nice gravy, season; then add the onion, the cabbage rolls, rest of the cabbage cut up fine, a few caraway seeds and cook slowly until done.
— Mrs. H. Eichelkraut.

SCALLOPED HAM

Cut raw ham into small pieces and place in baking dish. On top of ham, place small round potatoes. Season with pepper, pour in enough milk to cover potatoes and bake slowly about 1 hour.
— Alicia K. Steinhoff.

SCALLOPED HAM WITH VEGETABLES

Two slices ham, large potatoes sliced, 2 carrots sliced, 1 onion sliced, 1 bunch parsley, 1 pint milk, salt and pepper. Put layer of vegetables in buttered baking dish, then a layer of ham, rest of vegetables and cover with ham. Pour milk over all and bake in slow oven.
— Helen Lindau.

One Pan Pork Chop Dinner

Six or more lean pork chops, 6 medium sized peeled sweet or Irish potatoes, 6 onions if liked, 6 peeled, cored and halved apples, 1½ cups stock or boiling water. Put pork chops in roasting pan, arrange potatoes, onions and apples around and over them, add stock or water, season with salt and pepper and bake in moderate oven for fully 1½ hours. Turn vegetables and baste often.
— Mrs. E. S. Berndt.

Cauliflower with Sausages

Wash well and separate a cauliflower. Boil until tender, being careful to keep each floret whole. Then stir gently in a cream sauce until each peace is well coated. Put on round chop plate and surround with tiny sausages which have been baked or fried brown.
— Alicia K. Steinhoff.

Veal Goulash

Fry 1 tablespoon of chopped onion golden brown in 1 tablespoon of butter, add 1 pound of lean veal cut into inch pieces, ½ teaspoon salt, 1 teaspoon paprika, 1 tablespoon flour, and stir until slightly browned. Then add 1 cup of stock or water, cover and simmer for 1 hour. Add 1 cup of diced raw potatoes, cook 15 minutes longer and serve.
— Mrs. R. Albrecht.

Stewed Pork with Vegetables

Boil 2 pounds of lean pork about 30 minutes, then add 1 quart of more of carrots diced and boil about 30 minutes more. Then add 1 quart of more potatoes diced, 1 small onion cut fine, salt and pepper, and boil 30 minutes more until tender. Thicken with a little cornstarch dissolved in milk or water, or serve without thickening.
— Mrs. W. H. Jacobs.

Baked Hash

Butter a baking dish or casserole, put in a layer of sliced potatoes, then a layer of chopped meat left-overs and a few slices of onion; repeat alternately until all is used. Pour over all 2 well beaten eggs and enough milk to cover. Bake about 30 to 45 minutes.
— Olga T. Bohnsack.

Spanish Spaghetti

One package of spaghetti, 1 can of tomatoes, 2 large onions cut into small dice, 1 large green pepper cut into dice, 4 slices of bacon cut in squares, 1 pound of ground beef. Boil spaghetti in boiling salt water till tender; drain and blanch in cold water. Fry bacon in spider. Salt and pepper beef and shape into small balls, about size of walnut. Fry them in bacon grease; when meat is browned, add onions and peppers and fry about 15 minutes. Then pour with tomatoes over spaghetti which has been put in

sauce pan; let simmer 15 to 20 minutes. When serving sprinkle with grated cheese.
— Mrs. W. H. Mampe.

Sausage in Potato Boxes

Parboil the sausages 2 minutes, pricking them in a few places with a large darning needle. Arrange in a tin pan in a close row and set in the oven to finish cooking and brown. Press hot boiled potatoes through a ricer on to a heated platter and mold quickly with 2 spoons into a square shape, hollowing the center and making the sides straight. Drain the sausages and put in boxes, arranging in a row; serve hot. Garnish with fried tomatoes and a few sprigs of parsley.
— Mrs. E. S. Berndt.

Irish Stew

Take 1½ pounds each of beef and lamb, cut in cubes; put on to boil with enough water to cover and season to taste. Prepare 8 small sized onions, 6 small carrots, 12 potatoes, cut in cubes. When meat is partly done, skim carefully and add vegetables. Let stew until tender. Thicken gravy if desired.
— Mrs. Mandel Z.

Casey's Delight

Six carrots, 6 potatoes, 6 onions Cover with water and boil until done. Form 1 pound chopped round steak in balls size of an egg,

season and drop in stew; boil 10 minutes. Add 1 tablespoon flour, blend with 1 tablespoon butter.
— Helen Lindau.

Luncheon Corn Dish

One can corn
½ pound chopped (not ground) boiled ham
½ cup chopped celery
1 tablespoon chopped green pepper
salt and pepper

Mix all together with a thick white sauce, place in casserole and bake in oven. Garnish with sliced hard-boiled eggs.
— Lucia Koke Knowlton.

Hot Sweetbreads

Boil piece of green pepper, tops of some celery with 1 pound sweetbreads; let partly cool in water, then pick sweetbreads in small pieces, remove skin, and strain stock. Chop a cup of oysters fine; blend 2 tablespoons butter with flour and the strained stock, add ¾ cup cream; just boil up and fill in toasted bread squares made by hollowing out slices of bread of 2-inch thickness. Remove crust, leave ½-inch bottom and fill with sweetbreads. Serve with noodles and French peas, salt and pepper to taste; add a little onion salt.
— Ada Wilson Bohnsack.

Sautéed Kidney

Skin and core kidneys and cut them in slices. Melt 1 ounce butter in a pan and fry in this 1 onion minced. Put in the kidneys and fry for about 5 minutes, tossing them occasionally. Sprinkle in rather less than 1 ounce of flour, stir it all for 3 or 4 minutes longer; add 1 gill brown stock, ½ cup vinegar, and stir until it boils, then simmer gently for 10 minutes. Serve on a wall of mashed potatoes with sauce around. Beef kidneys will answer for this dish, only requiring to simmer longer in the gravy.
— Mrs. E. S. Berndt.

Stuffed Peppers a La Josephine

Mix well together 1 pound chopped beef, salt-pork cut in cubes, ¼ teaspoon cloves, ½ teaspoon white pepper, 1 teaspoon salt, and ½ cup raw rice. Cut the tops off 6 green peppers, remove seeds, and stuff with the mixture. Make meat balls out of the filling that is left. Into an iron pot put 1 tablespoon butter, 1 tablespoon flour, an onion, and let brown. Then add 1 cup water; when smooth add 1 can strained tomatoes. Put the peppers and meat balls in the gravy and let simmer for 1 hour.
— Mrs. O' Rourke.

Vegetables

Asparagus Pudding

Twenty-five spears of asparagus
3 eggs
8 tablespoons flour
2 large tablespoons butter
2 large tablespoons minced ham
3 tablespoons milk
salt and pepper

Break off the green heads as far as it is tender in ½ inch pieces, add the beaten eggs, sift in the flour, add ham, mix in the butter which must be melted but not hot, a little at a time, add milk and seasoning. Pour into well-buttered mold, tie up carefully and plunge into boiling water. Boil 2 hours. Water must be kept boiling constantly. Will serve 4 or 5 persons. Excellent with roast meat.
— Mrs. F. Ingham.

Creamed Asparagus

Three tablespoons butter, when melted add 2½ tablespoons flour, ½ teaspoon salt and a few grains cayenne. When smooth add 1 cup milk slowly, stirring until sauce is boiled. Then add
1 can asparagus tips cut in pieces and the liquor from the can, 4 hard boiled eggs, cut lengthwise and 1 pimento cut in squares. — Olga T. Bohnsack.

Steamed Fried Cabbage

Fifteen minute dish. Chop cabbage fine, fry some good bacon, remove the slices, then put the cabbage in the bacon grease. Cook, stirring often. When done, add ½ cup of cream. Serve hot.
— Mrs. Anna A. Jaekel.

Princess Cabbage

Boil a cabbage 15 minutes in boiling water, drain, add fresh water and boil until tender. Then chop fine, add 3 tablespoons milk, or cream, 1 tablespoon butter, 2 beaten eggs, salt and pepper. Mix well and bake brown.
— Helen Lindau.

Red Cabbage

Cut 1 head cabbage fine, add 3 good sized sour apples, which have been peeled and chopped fine, enough water to cover, ½ pound lean bacon, ¼ cup vinegar, ¼ cup sugar, and let simmer from 2 1/2 to 3 hours. Eat with pork roast.
— Mrs. A. Piepho.

Red Cabbage (French Style)

Choose a medium sized, very firm head of cabbage and shave it up as for cold slaw. In a large sauce pan put 2 tablespoons butter, one scant tablespoon sugar, ½ of a cup of vinegar, 6 cloves (tied in a piece of muslin), 1 teaspoon salt, and ¼ teaspoon pepper. When steaming add the cabbage, cover closely and cook until tender, about 1 hour.
— Mrs. Albrecht.

Stuffed Cabbage

After cutting out the root and heart from a good sized cabbage head, pick off several of the outer leaves and boil the remainder in salted water for 10 to 12 minutes; then remove it from the fire, open the leaves carefully, so as not to break them; then season the cabbage with salt and pepper, and fill the insides of the leaves with a nice stuffing or sausage force meat. Close them up, and tie the cabbage so that none of the stuffing escapes; then lay it in a pan; add 1 cup of carrots, 1 cup of onions, a piece of pork, and 1 cupful of white broth. Cover with a little fat from the soup stock; lay a buttered paper on top and let cook for 1 hour in Oven, basting it occasionally.
— Mrs. R. Albrecht.

Austrian Carrots

Scrape 1 quart carrots and cut into match sticks; then boil in salted water till tender. Drain off the water, add ½ cup vinegar, ¾ cup sugar and 1 large tablespoon butter. Cook the carrots

until they have a clear, transparent appearance; then serve.
— Alicia K. Steinhoff.

Sweet Corn Pudding

One can sweet corn, 3 eggs beaten light, 3 tablespoons melted butter, ½ cup milk, 2 tablespoons flour, salt and pepper. Pour mixture in buttered baking dish and bake in a hot oven I of an hour. — Mrs. R. J. Frank.

Fried Corn

Cut the corn from the cob and fry in a little butter, stir often, add salt and pepper and when nicely browned add a little cream. Do not boil after the cream is added.

Corn Fritters

One can corn, 1 cup flour, 2 eggs, 1 teaspoon baking powder, 1 teaspoon salt. Sift flour, salt and baking powder together, beat the eggs and add them to corn, add flour and drop by spoonfuls in hot fat. Fry until brown and serve hot.
— Miss Clara Wollerman.

Eggplant

One medium sized eggplant, 1 large onion, 1 tomato, 1 or 2 white tender sprays of celery, ½ cup of rice, lump of butter the size of an egg. Cut the eggplant into small pieces and boil 10

minutes, drain thoroughly, then add the onion, celery and tomato, chopped as fine as possible ; then add the rice and about a quart of water boiling hot. Cook about 1½ hours, then add the butter and a little salt and pepper to taste, then let it simmer for 20 minutes.
— Mrs. D. Wagner.

Eggplant Pudding

Take 1½ pounds of beef, pork or veal chopped and 2 eggplants. Cut egg plants in slices, salt, dredge in flour, and fry them. Put a layer of egg plant in a pan, then a layer of meat and continue till it is all used. Add either fresh or canned tomatoes, strained, salt and pepper and roast in oven.
— Mrs. Roth.

Stuffed Eggplant

Cut a good sized egg plant into halves and scoop out the center, leaving a wall ½ inch in thickness. To the portion taken out add 3 peeled tomatoes and chop together. Season with 1 teaspoon finely chopped onion 1 teaspoon salt, ¼ teaspoon pepper, a pinch of nutmeg and 2 tablespoons of fine bread crumbs. Fill the shells with the mixture, pour over each half 1 tablespoon melted butter, sprinkle with bread crumbs and bake | hour in a moderate oven.
— Mrs. R. Albrecht.

Creamed Macaroni

Put 1½ cups broken macaroni in boiling, salted water and boil 20 minutes. Remove from fire, add 1 tablespoon grated cheese, a little pepper, butter size of an egg, and 1 cup boiling milk. Bake in hot oven for 30 minutes and serve in vegetable dishes. Cut 2 hard boiled eggs in two, place a half on each dish in center of macaroni and sprinkle cut parsley around egg. This will serve 4 persons.
— Mrs. M. Eckhart.

Potato Puff

Two cups cold mashed potatoes. Beat to a white cream with 2 tablespoons melted butter. Add 2 eggs whipped very light and a scant 2 cups of cream or milk, salting to taste. Beat all well, pour into dish and bake in hot oven until nicely browned. Should come out light, puffy and delectable.
— Mrs. E. H. Pierce.

Potato Balls

For this you will need a vegetable cutter. Select large potatoes, pare them and press the vegetable cutter in one end of the potato. When all are cut, soak them in cold water a few minutes; drain, drop them into gently boiling water and cook 12 minutes. Drain off the water, add 1 tablespoon butter, a little salt and pepper and toss the potatoes over the fire until covered with the melted butter. Sprinkle with minced parsley and serve very hot.
— Mrs. E. S. Berndt.

A Toothsome Potato Dish

Slice a large white onion into a vegetable dish; lay on the slices of onion hot boiled potatoes sliced ; put on the potatoes a layer of bacon fried crisp. Pour over all 4 tablespoons hot bacon grease, set in the oven for only a few minutes, then serve.
— Mrs. E, S. Berndt.

Quick Potatoes

Peel potatoes, slice very thin and drop into boiling water. Let boil 10 minutes; drain, add salt, pepper, a little butter and ¼ or ½ cup hot cream according to quantity of potatoes. Chopped parsley may also be added. Serve at once. — Alicia K. Steinhoff.

Sweet Potatoes with Cream

Wash and scrub 4 large sweet potatoes and boil them. When done scrape off the skin, cut into quarters or eighths and put them in a saucepan with 1 heaping tablespoon butter, ¼ teaspoon salt, ¼ teaspoon pepper, 1 tablespoon sugar and ½ cup of rich cream. Cover closely and stand at the side of the fire for 15 minutes, shaking frequently.
— Mrs. R. Albrecht.

Candied Sweet Potatoes

Wash, scrub and parboil the potatoes. Scrape off the skin and cut them into ½-inch slices. Arrange in layers in a greased baking dish, putting over each layer bits of butter, a pinch of salt, a little granulated sugar and a few drops of water. For a good dishful about ⅔ of a cup of sugar, 2 tablespoons butter and 2 tablespoons water will be needed. Bake slowly in a moderate oven until they are browned on top and candied all through ; this will take about an hour.
— Mrs. R. Albrecht.

Stuffed Peppers

Choose red or green peppers of even size and of round rather than long shape. Cut off the tops, remove seeds and veins, cover with boiling water and parboil for 5 minutes. Drain, fill with the stuffing, arrange in a baking dish, pour in any good stock ½ inch deep and bake 30 minutes in a hot oven.

Stuffing. — Chop very fine sufficient cold roast chicken to make ¾ cupful. Add 1½ cups soaked bread crumbs, 1 large tomato skinned and cut fine or ½ cup canned tomato, ½ medium sized onion chopped fine, 1 heaping tablespoon butter melted, 1 tablespoon chopped parsley, 1 raw egg , and a scant ½ teaspoon salt.
— Mrs. R. Albrecht.

Stuffed Green Peppers

Six large green peppers, 1 pound chopped beef, ½ pound chopped pork. Cut tops off peppers, remove seeds and white pulp. Put them in dish, scald with hot water and let stand 10 minutes. Add a little soaked white bread to keep meat together and stuff peppers with the mixture. Cook 1 hour in following sauce:

 Melt, but do not brown, 1 tablespoon butter, add 1 heaping cooking spoon flour, 1 can tomatoes, 2 tablespoons sugar and salt to taste. Put peppers in sauce and add enough water to float peppers in pot.
— Mrs. R. Liss.

Green Peas with Bacon

Two quarts shelled green peas, 2 onions, 1 handful parsley, 2 pounds bacon, 2 tablespoons flour, two glasses water, salt and pepper to taste. Cut the bacon in dices and brown in a sauce pan ; sprinkle with flour ; then add the water, peas, onions (whole), parsley (tied), and cook for 50 minutes. When done take out onions and parsley and serve.

Turnip Cups with Peas

Steam or boil medium sized turnips till tender; scoop out center until only a shell remains. Have ready green peas cooked tender or use canned peas, to which have been added butter, salt and pepper. Fill the turnip cups with peas and pour over all a white sauce. Carrots may be used instead of turnips. Use the scooped out portion in soup or vegetable salad.
— Alicia K. Steinhoff.

Rice and Cheese

One-half cup rice, ¼ pound American cheese, ½ cup strained tomatoes, a few bread crumbs. Cook rice in salt water. When tender place a layer in pan, then a layer of cheese cubes, another layer of rice, tomatoes, dot top with butter, sprinkle with bread crumbs and bake 20 minutes in a rather hot oven. Serve hot.
— Mrs. W. Schilke.

Swiss Chard

Wash ½ peck Swiss chard till clean and let stand in cold water for 3 to 4 hours. Then boil for 25 minutes, drain and chop fine. Cut salt pork or bacon in cubes and fry brown. Pour drippings and cubes over Swiss chard and serve. Spinach can also be prepared in this way.
— Josephine O' Rourke.

Baked Tomatoes

Wash 6 tomatoes, cut a thin slice from the stem end and scoop out all the pulp. Sprinkle the inside of tomatoes with salt. Mix the pulp with 6 crackers rolled fine, salt and pepper to taste and onions chopped fine, if liked. Fill the tomatoes with this mixture, place ½ teaspoon butter on top of each and bake from 15 to 20 minutes. Garnish with boiled rice and the melted butter left from baked tomatoes.
— Mrs. F. Kasang.

STUFFED TOMATOES

Use firm ripe tomatoes. Wash and wipe them dry, and cut a small hole in the blossom end and remove the inside, being careful not to break the sides. Mince finely some boiled or roasted chicken or veal, add the tomato pulp, chopped nuts, a little celery and onion, and season with salt, cayenne, lemon juice and parsley; and add sufficient bread crumbs to make a rather stiff mixture. Stuff the tomatoes with the mixture, place in well buttered pan, and bake until tender, basting with melted butter. Dish carefully and garnish with parsley.
— Mrs. Hunt.

FILLED TOMATOES

Twelve ripe, firm tomatoes, 1 pound chopped meat (pork and beef), 1 tablespoon raw rice, 1 onion, a little parsley cut fine, 1 or 2 eggs, salt and pepper. Wash tomatoes, cut top open, but not off, leaving a lid, scoop out insides; put pulp taken out in pan and stew. Mix meat, onion, rice, eggs and seasoning together and fill the tomatoes, but not too full. Push down lid and set all in a large kettle with a wide bottom. Brown 2 tablespoons butter, 2 heaping tablespoons flour with a little onion; add the tomatoes that have been stewing and stir until smooth. Strain and pour over the filled tomatoes; simmer very slowly until done. Add a little more water if needed and seasoning. Do not stir but give the kettle a few turns so it will not burn.
— Mrs. G. Lemar.

MEATLESS LOAF

One cup chopped carrots, 1 cup bread crumbs, 1 cup chopped nuts, 1 cup chopped tomatoes. Season to taste, put in bread pan and bake ½ hour.
— Mrs. O. T. Bohnsack.

Salads

Thousand Island Dressing

One egg yolk, pinch of salt, cup of oil, 3 tablespoons chili sauce, 1 green pepper. Beat egg thoroughly, add oil slowly and continue beating constantly in one direction. Thin with cream and add chili sauce and peppers chopped fine.
— Mrs. H. Trippler.

Thousand Island Dressing

Two teaspoons Worcestershire sauce, 2 teaspoons ketchup, 2 teaspoons sugar, 2 teaspoons of vinegar, a pinch of salt. Shake in paprika, ¼ cup of olive oil, small piece of ice.
— Johanna Kretchmer.

Mayonnaise Dressing

To the yolks of 4 eggs add slowly 4 tablespoons oil, then 4 tablespoons vinegar. Stir over the fire until it thickens ; when cooled add 4 tablespoons oil, 1 teaspoon salt, 2 teaspoons sugar, mustard to taste and lastly 1 cup whipped cream. Butter may be used instead of oil. This makes quite a little.
— Mrs. H. G. Tischer.

French Dressing

Rub the bowl with a bruised clove of garlic ; add ½ teaspoon salt, ⅛ teaspoon pepper, ¼ teaspoon paprika, and 6 tablespoons olive oil. Beat thoroughly, then add 2 to 3 tablespoons vinegar slowly and continue beating until thickened. A piece of ice put into the bowl while stirring will aid in chilling the mixture.
— Alicia K. Steinhoflf.

Spanish Dressing

To a French Dressing add 1 mild green pepper finely chopped, and 2 tablespoons finely chopped Spanish onion.
— Alicia K. Steinhoff.

Russian Salad Dressing

To a French Dressing add the yolks of 2 hard boiled eggs chopped, 1 green pepper chopped, and 1 tablespoon ketchup. Just before serving beat hard for a few minutes.
— Alicia K. Steinhoff.

Fruit Salad Dressing

Beat 4 egg yolks with ½ cup honey and the grated rind and juice of 1 lemon until light. Put in double boiler and boil until thick; when nearly cold add 12 marshmallows cut in pieces. Let stand until cold. When ready to serve add ½ pint whipping cream which has been whipped stiff.
— Mrs. W. Mampe.

Fruit Salad Dressing

One egg, 2 tablespoons sugar, 2 tablespoons lemon juice, and 2 tablespoons pineapple or orange juice. Beat the egg, add sugar and fruit juices and cook in a double boiler, stirring constantly until thickened. Cool and combine with salad. Excellent with any combination of fruits.
— Mrs. H. A. Zorn.

Fruit Salad Dressing

The juice of 3 lemons, juice of 2 oranges, 3 eggs, ½ cup sugar. Boil slowly till clear and add 1 cup whipped cream. Delicious.
— Mrs. Chas. North.

Salad Dressing

One-half teaspoon paprika, ¼ teaspoon salt, ¼ teaspoon black pepper, 2 teaspoons powdered sugar, 2 tablespoons olive oil, 3 tablespoons vinegar. Mix together and chill with ice before adding vinegar.
— Mrs. F. Neyendorf.

Cream Dressing

Mix 1 teaspoon of salt, 1 teaspoon of flour, 1 teaspoon of mustard, 1 tablespoon of sugar, and 2 tablespoons of butter. Then add the beaten yolks of 2 eggs, ¾ cup cream and lastly ¼ cup vinegar ; cook over hot water until it thickens. Chill before using.
— Mrs. Anna A. Jaekel.

Non Pareil Salad Dressing

Yolks of 8 eggs well beaten, 1 cupful of white sugar, ½ cup of rich cream, 1 tablespoon of mustard, 1 tablespoon salt, 1 tablespoon pepper. Mix thoroughly, then put over fire 1½ pints vinegar and ½ cupful butter. If vinegar is too strong dilute with water. Let boil, then pour over the other ingredients, stirring all the time. Put back over the fire and let boil for 15 minutes.
-Mrs. Hunt.

Salad Dressing

Yolks of 4 eggs beaten light, 1 tablespoon sugar, scant tablespoon salt, scant tablespoon mustard, pinch of red pepper. Mix with ½ cup weak vinegar, stir with the eggs. Cook in double boiler; while hot, add butter size of a walnut. When cold add ½ cup cream.
— Mrs. R. Baur.

Boiled Salad Dressing

One tablespoon butter, 1 tablespoon flour, 1 tablespoon sugar, 1 teaspoon salt, 1 teaspoon mustard, ½ cup vinegar, 1 cup milk, 3 eggs. Melt the butter and add the flour, stir until it is smooth, add the milk, let it come to a boil, stirring constantly. Add the seasoning to the eggs and beat them, add the vinegar a little at a time. Add this to the other ingredients and cook in a double boiler until it thickens. Use it cold.
— Clara Rauschert.

BOILED SALAD DRESSING

Two eggs, ½ cup vinegar, ½ cup water, ½ cup sugar, 1 heaping teaspoon dry mustard and 1 heaping teaspoon cornstarch. Boil until thick. After removing from fire add a good sized piece of butter. Thin with cream as used.
— Mrs. H. A. Zorn.

SALAD DRESSING

Two well beaten eggs, 2 tablespoons of sugar, ½ cup of vinegar, ½ cup of water mixed with 1 tablespoon melted butter. Beat hard, boil until thick.
— Mrs. G. Massman.

BOILED SALAD DRESSING

One cup vinegar, add a little water, 1 teaspoon mustard, 2 tablespoons flour scant, 2 eggs, separate ; butter size of an egg, sugar to taste and a little salt. Mix the mustard, flour, salt and sugar, add the beaten yolks of eggs, then add vinegar and boil in double boiler until thick. After it is off the fire, add beaten whites of eggs.
— Mrs. E. Koretke.

Adirondack Salad

One can peas, ¼ pound cheese, any kind, 2 large onions, six large pickles, sour or dill. Strain peas, dice cheese, onions and pickles (sugar pickles, if sour), and mix with mayonnaise dressing.
— Mrs. C. F. Teuchert.

Alsatian Salad

Cook 3 frankfurter sausages for a few minutes in boiling water. Chill these and cut into very thin slices. Slice 4 medium size cold potatoes and 1 small white onion, half a dozen firm pickles and stir this mixture lightly with 4 tablespoons of French dressing.
— Mrs. A. Steging.

Ruby Apple Salad

Make a syrup of 3 cups sugar and 3 cups water, to which add enough red stick candy or red cinnamon drops to give a rich red color. When candy is dissolved add 8 to 10 sweet apples, peeled and cored, and simmer slowly until apples are tender and ruby colored. Drain and cool ; fill center with chopped nuts and celery, place on lettuce leaves, and pour a fruit salad dressing over them. Pears may also be used this way.
— Mrs. W. C. Hinrichs.

Asparagus and Tomato Salad

Chill as many tomatoes as needed ; skin and scoop out center. Chill on ice till very firm. Have ready asparagus tips about 3 inches long. Dust the inside of tomatoes with salt and pepper, then stand 4 or 5 tips in each tomato. Place on lettuce and pour over each a mayonnaise or boiled dressing.
— Alicia K. Steinhoff.

Banana Salad

Peel bananas and cut each into 4 parts, lengthwise. Roll each part in lemon juice, then in finely chopped nuts. Pile log cabin fashion on lettuce leaves and pour over it a mayonnaise or boiled dressing.
— Alicia K. Steinhoff.

Bean Celery Salad

One pint of pork and beans, 4 tablespoons celery cut in small pieces, 2 tablespoons finely chopped onion, ¼ cup salad dressing mixed with ¼ cup whipped cream. Serve on lettuce and garnish with olives.
— Mrs. R. Baur.

Beet Salad

Take 4 or 5 good sized pickled beets and chop or cut up in small pieces, some English celery cut up in small pieces and mix with pepper and salt, place in a salad bowl. Now take 4 hard boiled eggs, chop the whites up and place in circle around the edge of the bowl. Take the yellow and mash with fork and place in center. Garnish with celery leaves.

Dressing. — 2 eggs beaten, 1 tablespoon olive oil, salt and pepper, 1 tablespoon vinegar. Beat together and pour on salad.
— Mrs. R. Albrecht.

Cabbage and Beet Salad

Chop a medium sized head of cabbage fine and add to it half as many chopped beets, boiled and allowed to cool. To 2 quarts of this mixture add a 1 cup of horseradish or a 5¢ bottle. Put in white sugar and salt to taste. Cover all with vinegar and allow it to stand for 24 hours before serving.
— Mrs. A. Steging.

Cold Slaw Salad

Wash a cabbage and lay in iced water, slightly salted for an hour or two. Then drain, cut into shreds, adding a stalk of celery, and 3 apples (also cut into bits). Then cover all with a cream dressing.
— Mrs. Anna A. Jaekel.

Celery Salad

Mash a cream cheese, add chopped nuts, salt, and moisten with boiled dressing, stuff the mixture into the hollow part of crisp celery. Serve as usual or cut up in inch pieces and serve on lettuce with boiled dressing.
— Alicia K. Steinhoff.

Celery Salad

Cut celery into small pieces, add walnuts and mix with cream salad dressing. Add dressing just before serving else it will get watery.
— Mrs. W. H. Jacobs.

Cassaba Melon

Cut Cassaba melon in shape of banana or in heart shapes; put finely chopped white grapes (can be bought, seeded, in cans for salad) around edge, in center put pomegranate seeds. Serve with French dressing.
— Ada Wilson Bohnsack.

Chicken Salad

Boil a chicken tender; skin and cut all meat into small pieces. Cut up 2 large stalks celery, 1 can peas, 1 sweet red pepper cut fine; mix and add mayonnaise dressing. Serve on lettuce leaves.
— Mrs. Sodemann.

Chicken Salad

Cut cold chicken in dice, add half as much celery and serve with a boiled dressing.
— Mrs. Mandel Z.

Chicken Salad

One fine large chicken boiled tender and chopped, 12 eggs boiled hard, 6 stuffed pickled peppers chopped, 1 cup melted butter or salad oil ; 3 cups chopped celery, 1 teaspoon ground pepper, 2 tablespoons black mustard ground, 1 cup vinegar. Rub the yolks of the eggs with the butter or salad oil. If the chicken is fat, the oil taken from the water in which it is boiled is better than the salad oil. Chop the whites of the eggs. Put all the ingredients together, and work it until it is thoroughly mixed. If you cannot get the celery use white cabbage, and put celery seed in the cup of vinegar that you are going to use and let it stand over night. Other pickles can be used with some pepper sauce instead of the stuffed peppers. This recipe will make nearly a gallon of salad and will keep for days in a cool place.
— Mrs. R. Albrecht.

Mock Chicken Salad

Two pounds veal from the leg, boil in one piece until done, let cool. Cut in dice. Measure meat and add an equal amount of celery, cut in dice. Dressing. — ⅔ cup vinegar, ⅓ cup water, ½ cup sugar, 1 teaspoon salt, 1 teaspoon mustard, 1 tablespoon

flour, 2 eggs. Mix thoroughly and cook in double boiler until thick. When cool stir in a cup of cream and add to the salad. Serve on lettuce leaves.
— Miss Clara Mertz.

COMBINATION SALAD

Four ripe tomatoes, 1 can white asparagus, 2 stalks celery, small, 1 green pepper. Cut tomatoes in slices, dice celery and peppers. Serve on lettuce leaf and cover with boiled or mayonnaise dressing.
— Mrs. H. Trippler.

COMBINATION SALAD

One can peas, 2 stalks celery cut fine, 1 sweet red pepper cut fine, 6 hard boiled eggs cut in pieces. Mix with mayonnaise.
— Mrs. Sodemann.

CRAB MEAT A LA CARDINAL

Shred crab meat, add cut up celery, a little onion, minced green pepper, and seasoning to taste. Cut white bread in circles, place one round of bread on a lettuce leaf, place a hollowed out tomato, or a thick slice of tomato, on bread; fill tomato with the crab mixture and pour over all a mayonnaise dressing.
— Alicia K. Steinhoflf.

Date Salad

To 2 apples take 1 banana and i cup dates ; cut all in small pieces. Add a little lemon and orange juice and mix with dressing to which whipped cream has been added.
— Miss L. Gansz.

Egg Salad

Shred crisp lettuce leaves, place on salad plates, then lay slices of hard boiled egg on the lettuce and grate cheese over all. Dust with paprika and serve with French dressing.
— Mrs. H. F. Rente.

Egg Salad

One dozen boiled eggs, 1 can pimentos, 1 large bottle stuffed olives, 5 cents worth of sweet pickles, 1 small onion. Chop each ingredient separately, then mix and serve with white sauce.

White Sauce. — To 2 tablespoons butter, melted, add 2 tablespoons flour, ¼ teaspoon salt, a little pepper, and 1 cup milk. Let cook till thick.
— Mrs. Mandel Z.

Egg Salad with Salmon Mayonnaise

Hard boil 6 or 8 eggs, remove shells and chill on ice. Rub ¼ cup of canned salmon to a paste, add to 1 cup of mayonnaise

or boiled dressing into which has been beaten ¼ cup cream. Arrange crisp lettuce hearts in a nest on a shallow serving dish. Cut eggs in eighths, pile them in center, sprinkle with salt and pepper and pour over the prepared mayonnaise. Sprinkle with finely chopped chives or paprika.
— Alicia K. Steinhoff.

Golden Salad

Cut 4 hard boiled eggs in halves lengthwise, and to the mashed yolks add 1 teaspoon melted butter, 2 teaspoons mayonnaise dressing, 1 tablespoon ham ground fine, and salt. Form into balls and fill space in each white. Arrange on lettuce.
— Mrs. O. A. Skibbe.

Fish Salad

Boil white fish, let cool, bone ; mix with celery and cucumbers and serve with dressing on lettuce leaves.
— Mrs. R.
Meyer.

Fruit Salad

One pound grapes seeded and peeled, ½ pound walnuts, add a little celery cut in small pieces, add apples cut fine to taste. Mix with mayonnaise dressing.
— Mrs. F. Nyendorf.

FRUIT SALAD

One can sliced pineapples, 1 can pears, 1 pound white grapes, 3 oranges, and 2 boxes marshmallows. Mix with fruit salad dressing to which whipped cream has been added.
— Mrs. H. Trippler.

WHIPPED CREAM FRUIT SALAD

Two cups seeded white grapes, 2 cups chopped apples, 1 cup celery, 1 cup chopped walnuts, 1 cup marshmallows, cut in pieces, 1½ cup candied cherries. Whip 1 quart of cream, sweetened slightly, add the juice of 1 lemon. Add dressing just before serving.
— Mrs. A. L. Dunfrund.

FRUIT SALAD

Twenty-four marshmallows, 1 can pineapple, 2 juicy apples, 6 oranges, lettuce leaves, 1 can white cherries may be added. Cut fruit and marshmallows into small pieces, then mix and chill. For dressing use 1 tablespoon butter, pinch of salt, 2 tablespoons sugar, 2 tablespoons vinegar, 2 eggs, ½ pint of whipped cream. Beat up eggs in double boiler add vinegar, sugar and salt and butter, then cook until thick. Cool and add whipped cream. Mix with fruit and serve on lettuce leaves.
— Mrs. R. Baur.

Hanoverian Salad

Three medium sized beets, 2 cooked potatoes, ⅓ pound cooked ham, 1 small onion, several stalks celery. Chop ingredients fine, mix with cream dressing. Serve on bed of lettuce and garnish with hard boiled eggs.
— Mrs. Wm. Bohnsack.

Herring Salad Appetizer

Lay 5 to 6 salt herring in fresh water over night. The next morning clean them and cut in small pieces. Cut up 3 pounds cooked veal, 3 to 4 hard boiled eggs, 4 cooked beets, 2 large apples, pepper, a good i cup vinegar (if strong mix with a little water), a little dry mustard and one tablespoon sugar. No salt. Stir well together then put it in a covered jar for a day.
— Mrs. O. Kleppisch.

Herring Salad

Clean and remove bones from 2 salt herring ; cut fine. Cut in small pieces ,1 little onion, a bunch of celery, 3 hard boiled eggs, 4 boiled potatoes, 1 cucumber, and add 1 cup peas. Mix all together and add 3 tablespoons vinegar. Line a bowl with lettuce and fill with the salad.
— Mrs. W. Brockschmidt.

Herring Salad

This is a very palatable and also economical salad recipe, as it can be prepared from all kinds of left-overs. Take 4 salted herring that have been soaked for several hours before using, skin and bone them; 1½ pounds cold boiled meat (soup meat preferred), about half this amount of cold boiled potatoes, 1 boiled celery root, 1 onion, 2 good sized pickles, 2 apples, and run all through the food chopper. Add any kind of meat gravy or extract, about ½ glass of any kind of jelly, 2 teaspoons prepared mustard, scant ½ teaspoon pepper. Mix all this thoroughly, put into a large salad dish, and garnish top with four hard boiled eggs (yolks and whites chopped separately for the center). Use enough chopped pickled beets and pickles to go around the edge.
— Mrs. A. Streger.

Italian Salad

Lax ham, boiled ham, veal tongue, mortadella, servelat sausage or any kind of sausage, also beets and celery. Mix with mayonnaise.
— Mrs. H. G. Tischer.

Kidney Bean Salad

One onion size of an egg, 3 sour pickles, 5 cents worth of walnuts, 1 can kidney beans, mayonnaise dressing.
— Mrs. Emil C. Weihe.

KIDNEY BEAN SALAD

One can shrimps, 1 can kidney beans, and celery to suit taste. Mix with mayonnaise dressing.
— Mrs. W. C. Pfister.

LETTUCE SALAD

Take as many heads of lettuce as needed. Cut lettuce fine, then cut in slices 2 bunches radishes, 10 small onions, and 1 cucumber ; salt a little. Put in layers in a dish and dress with oil and vinegar or with mayonnaise.
— Mrs. O'Rourke.

LETTUCE SALAD WITH CREAM DRESSING

1 cup of thick, sweet cream, add ⅔ tablespoon vinegar and ½ cup sugar. Mix thoroughly with lettuce. Head-lettuce is best.
— Marie Doederlein.

LOBSTER SALAD

Two cans lobster, 1 green pepper, 3 stalks celery, ½ can pimentos. Mix all together and serve on lettuce leaf with dressing. Salmon and shrimp may also be used in the same way.
— Mrs. H. Trippler.

Peach Salad

Arrange halves of fine large peaches, hollow side up on salad plates covered with lettuce or endive, chop hearts of celery and almonds ; moisten with mayonnaise and fill in cavity of peach. Cover with another half peach to resemble a whole peach, cover with mayonnaise, and over this a rather soft cranberry jelly. Sprinkle with parsley.
— Mrs. O. Kleppisch.

Pepper Salad

Roast sweet peppers, then peel, and salt. Let stand a few minutes, then add oil and vinegar.
— Mrs. Roth.

Perfection Salad

Two tablespoons Knox's gelatine, ½ cup water, ½ cup vinegar, juice of 1 lemon, 1 pint boiling water, ½ cup sugar, 1 teaspoon salt, 1 can peas, 6 sweet-sour pickles, 1 cup chopped celery, J cup pimentos. Soften gelatine in cold water ; mix vinegar, lemon juice, sugar, salt and boiling water. Bring all to boiling point and add softened gelatine. Let cool when mixture begins to thicken add peas, celery, pimentos and pickles. Turn into large or individual molds. Chill and serve with mayonnaise dressing.
— Olga T. Bohnsack.

Perfection Salad

One envelope Knox Sparkling Gelatine, ½ cup cold water, ½ cup mild vinegar, 2 tablespoons lemon juice, 2 cups boiling water, ½ cup sugar, 1 teaspoon salt, 1 cup finely shredded cabbage, 2 cups celery cut in small pieces, 2 pimentoes. Soak gelatine in cold water 5 minutes; add vinegar, lemon juice, boiling water, sugar and salt. Strain and when mixture begins to thicken, add remaining ingredients. Turn into mold, first dipped in cold water and chill. Remove to a bed of lettuce or endive and garnish with mayonnaise or boiled dressing; or cut mixture into cubes and serve in cases made of red or green peppers.
— Ella Baerwald.

Pineapple Salad

Place a thin slice of pineapple on a lettuce leaf; spread cream cheese on the pineapple ; place star shaped pieces or strips of pimento on top, and serve with boiled dressing.
— Alicia K. Steinhoff.

Prune Salad

Soak prunes over night; next day cook them, but not too much. Take out stones and fill with walnut or pecan meats. Put lettuce leaves on salad plates, add 3 prunes and dressing on the side.

Dressing. — Boil together, stirring constantly, a small piece of butter size of a walnut, 1 egg well beaten, | teaspoon salt, 1 ta-

blespoon sugar, 1 scant teaspoon mustard, 3 tablespoons vinegar. When smooth let cool and then add ½ cup milk.
— Mrs. F. Kasang.

Salmon Salad

One can salmon cut in small pieces, 12 small cucumber pickles chopped, 1 very small head cabbage chopped fine, 2 eggs boiled hard and chopped. Mix all together thoroughly.

Salmon Salad

One can salmon, the skins and bones removed; 1 cup chopped celery, 1 grated onion, salt and pepper to taste.
Dressing. — One egg well beaten with | teaspoon mustard, salt and 1 tablespoon sugar; boil with ½ cup vinegar until it thickens, and add a lump of butter. Pour dressing, when cool, over the salmon, mixing it thoroughly. Line a dish with lettuce, pour the mixture on it. Chop a boiled beet fine, sprinkle on top, and edge with, sliced egg, hard boiled. This dish can be made in the morning and served any time during the day.
— Mrs. A. Steging.

Tongue Salad

Boil, skin, trim and slice, then cut in dice 1 fresh beef tongue. Add the whites of 6 hard boiled eggs, and 3 stalks of celery cut in small pieces, mix thoroughly with cream dressing and serve.

Cream Dressing. Beat the yolks of 2 eggs and work smooth with 1 tablespoon sugar, 1 teaspoon mustard, 8 tablespoons olive oil,

3 tablespoons vinegar, 1 teaspoon salt, a dash of cayenne pepper, and lastly 1 cup well whipped cream.
— Mrs. A. Piepho.

Stuffed Tomato Salad

After skinning tomatoes, scoop out insides and chop with chicken livers or chicken meat, black walnuts, celery, onions, mayonnaise, pepper and salt. Stuff the tomatoes and garnish with stiff mayonnaise.
— Alicia K. Steinholf.

Waldorf Salad

One quart chopped apples, 1 quart chopped celery, and 1 cup walnuts. Mix with this dressing: yolks of 4 eggs, butter size of an egg, 1 teaspoon salt, 1 teaspoon mustard flour, a little cayenne, ½ cup vinegar, 1 tablespoon sugar. Stir all well, put on stove to thicken, but don't let boil. When thick add 1 cup whipped cream, and mix with salad.
— Mrs. Mandel Z.

Waldorf Salad

One cup diced apples, 1 cup celery cut fine, 1 cup grape-nuts. Mix apples and celery with fruit salad dressing at once to prevent discoloration. Add grape-nuts and place on ice until serving time.
— Mrs. H. A. Zorn.

Sunday Night Salad

Cut cold roast veal in ½-inch cubes, there should be 2 cups; wash and scrape celery and cut in thin slices, there should be 1½ cups; chill until crisp in cold water, drain and dry. Remove stones from 4 olives and finely chop them. Parboil ½ red pepper 10 minutes, remove seeds and cut half the pepper in strips, the remainder in fancy shapes. Mix veal, celery, olives, pepper strips, and marinate with French dressing. Moisten with cream salad dressing, mound in a bowl and mask with dressing. Garnish with celery tips and peppers cut in fancy shapes and cucumber pickles cut in strips.
— Mrs. O. A. Skibbe.

Puddings and Desserts

Cream Sauce

One egg, ½ cup sugar, 1 tablespoon cornstarch. Whip this to a foam, then add 1 pint boiling milk ; boil until thick, lastly add 1 teaspoon vanilla.
— Miss L. Gansz.

Hard Sauce

One cup powdered sugar, ½ cup butter, 1 tablespoon cream, ⅔ teaspoon vanilla, ⅓ teaspoon lemon extract. Cream butter, add cream, sugar and flavoring.

Hard Sauce

Stir together 1 cup white sugar, ½ cup butter until creamy and light; add vanilla to taste or flavor with raspberry or strawberry juice. The froth of an egg beaten stiff.

Vanilla Sauce

Mix thoroughly ½ cup sugar, 1 tablespoon flour. Stir it into 1 cup boiling water. Let boil ; when clear add 2 tablespoons butter and 1 teaspoon vanilla. Beat until butter is melted.
— Alicia K. Steinhoff.

WINE SAUCE

Stir a heaping teaspoon of cornstarch into a little cold water to a smooth paste; add a cup of boiling water with one cup of sugar, a piece of butter size of an egg, boil together 10 minutes, remove from the fire, and when cool stir into it ½ cup of wine. — Mrs. O. Kleppisch.

ANGEL FOOD PUDDING

One small cup sugar, 2 eggs well beaten, 1 apple diced, ¼ cup seedless raisins dredged in 2 tablespoons of flour, 1 teaspoon baking powder, almond flavor to taste. Bake slowly 30 minutes and serve with whipped cream. This will serve 5 or 6 persons, as it is a very rich dessert.
— Mrs. Streger.

BAKED APPLE DUMPLINGS

Pare and core the apples. Make a baking powder biscuit dough, a trifle stiffer than for biscuits. Roll on floured board and cut in numbers of parts desired. Shape around apples after sprinkling each with sugar and cinnamon. Bake a golden brown and serve with any desired sauce such as a jelly sauce or whipped cream.
— Clara L. Kemnitz.

APPLE CUSTARD

Heat 1 cup water and ½ cup sugar, to boiling point. Drop into it 3 medium; sized apples peeled and sliced, cook slowly until apples are tender, then lift the pieces out and put in serving dish. Boil syrup down one half an pour over apples. Mix 1 tablespoon cornstarch, ¼ cup sugar, 1 egg, beaten well, 1 large cup milk; cook slowly until thick and pour around apples. Drop a little currant jelly in center.
— Mrs. H. England.

RUSSIAN APPLES

Wipe off, core and pare large sour apples. Put close together in a baking dish and fill each cavity with mince meat prepared as for pies, but without apples. Bake in a slow oven until apples are tender, and serve cold.
— Mrs. R. Albrecht.

BAKED APPLES

Cream ½ cup sugar with 1 tablespoon butter. Stir into 1 tablespoon flour the grated rind of 1 lemon ; mix with sugar and butter. Pour this mixture in the spaces left by coring 6 apples. Place in a moderate oven and bake till soft.
— Mrs. F. C. Kramer.

Baked Apples and Prunes

Core apples and fill with prunes chopped fine, using sugar to taste. Bake. Serve with whipped cream, if desired.
— Mrs. F. Schoenwolf.

Baked Apples

Core apples without peeling and place in a shallow pan. Fill center of apples with light brown sugar. Sprinkle a little cornstarch on bottom of pan, between apples, and pour on water to come up about a quarter of an inch around apples. Bake and serve with sauce that will be in the pan from the cornstarch, sugar and water.
— Mrs. Theo. Doering.

Apple Snow

Boil about 5 apples to a pulp, sweetening to taste. When cool place in a large bowl, together with the white of 1 egg, juice of 1 lemon, and 1 cup of sugar. Beat the mixture about 30 minutes with a wire egg beater. The result is three times the amount you started with, enough to serve 10 people.
— Mrs. Albrecht.

Apricot Whip

Boil 1 pound dried apricots till tender and sweeten to taste. When cool whip very smooth, add the stiffly beaten whites of 3 eggs and beat all well together. Serve with whipped cream or

with a custard made of the egg yolks and thickened with cornstarch.
— Mrs. Mandel Z.

Apricot Prune Dessert

Cook clear 1 cup tapioca in 2 quarts of boiling water, add 4 pound of prunes and ½ pound apricots. Sweeten to taste, about ½ cup sugar. Stir occasionally. When cold serve with cream.
— Mrs. O. Kleppisch.

Fruit Dessert

Wash and soak dried apricots, then simmer until soft. Add enough sugar to sweeten and put through a coarse strainer. Let stand until cold, then add bananas, cut fine, and serve with whipped cream.
— Mrs, W. Brockschmidt.

Bread Pudding

Grate about ¾ loaf of bread, cutting off the crust; pour over it about a quart of scalded milk; a piece of butter the size of an egg; when cool add a teaspoon cinnamon, ½ cup sugar, ½ cup raisins, and ¼ teaspoon baking soda dissolved in a little hot water. Beat 2 or 3 eggs very light and add last. Turn all in well greased pudding dish and bake 45 minutes. Serve with hard sauce. This recipe may be steamed or boiled.
— Mrs. O. Kleppisch.

CHOCOLATE BREAD PUDDING

Two cups stale bread crumbs, enough milk to cover, 2 eggs, ¾ cup sugar, 2 small squares chocolate. Mix well and bake 30 minutes; to be eaten with any kind of sauce.
— Mrs. Albrecht.

CARROT PUDDING

One cup flour, ½ cup sugar, salt; put through chopper 1 cup raw potatoes, 1 cup carrots, 1 cup suet, | teaspoon cloves, ½ teaspoon cinnamon, ½ teaspoon allspice, 1 cup raisins, ½ cup currants, ½ teaspoon baking soda. Steam 2 hours. Serve with lemon sauce.

LEMON SAUCE. — Yolk of 2 eggs, 1 cup sugar, ½ cup butter, 1 tablespoon cornstarch, juice of 1 lemon. Stir this into 1½ cups boiling water and cook a few minutes.
— Mrs. Sodemann.

CARAMEL CUP CUSTARD

One-half cup sugar, ½ cup boiling water, 2 eggs, salt, 2 cups scalded milk, vanilla. Melt sugar slowly over fire, then add water and let boil until clear. Pour into each of 4 cups. Scald milk. Beat eggs slightly. Add to milk. Add vanilla. Pour into cups containing syrup. Place in pan of hat water and bake until set.
— Mary Sternberg.

Coconut Pudding

One-half cup sugar, 2 egg yolks, 1 cup milk, 1 teaspoon lemon extract, 4 cup bread crumbs, 2 tablespoons or more of coconut. Bake about 30 minutes Make frosting of the whites of eggs and ¼ cup of sugar. Brown slightly in oven.
— Mrs. O. Kleppisch.

Cornstarch Pudding

One pint milk, 2 tablespoons cornstarch, 3 tablespoons sugar and a little salt, whites of 3 eggs beaten. When milk is boiling add sugar, then add starch dissolved in cold milk, and then eggs whipped to a stiff froth. Cook a few minutes then add some coconut and set in a cool place.

Sauce. — 1 pint boiled milk, 3 tablespoons sugar, yolks of 3 eggs mixed with sugar. Then add to boiling milk. Flavor with vanilla.
— Mrs. J. Semmlow.

Chocolate Cornstarch Pudding

One pint milk, 4 tablespoons chocolate, 2 tablespoons cornstarch, ½ cup sugar, ¼ teaspoon salt. Melt chocolate, heat the milk to boiling. Add sugar, salt and chocolate. Mix the corn starch with 2 tablespoons of water, add to the boiling milk. Boil for 2 minutes. Cook in double boiler for 20 minutes. Wet the mold with cold water, turn the pudding into it, chill and serve with sugar and cream.
— Clara Rauschert.

Chocolate Pudding

One pint milk, 10 tablespoons grated bread, 5 tablespoons grated chocolate, 4 eggs, butter size of an egg, 1 small cup sugar. Mix crumbs and chocolate with a little of the milk, add yolks of eggs and sugar, put rest of the milk on fire, let come to a boil and stir in the mixture, add butter and cook until thick like cream, stirring constantly, then put in buttered pudding dish. Beat the whites of eggs to froth, add 3 tablespoons powdered sugar, ½ teaspoon cornstarch, pour over pudding and brown in hot oven.
— Mrs. Wm. Fredericks.

Fig Pudding

Three eggs, ⅔ cup granulated sugar, ½ cup butter, 1 cup bread crumbs, ½ cup chopped figs or dates. Mix together butter, sugar, beaten yolks of eggs, figs, crumbs, and lastly froth of eggs. Turn into a well greased pan and bake in a moderate oven for 35 minutes, or until firm to the touch. If steaming is preferred, turn into a covered mold and steam 24 hours. Serve with wine sauce or any pudding sauce.
— Mrs. O. Kleppisch.

Five Minute Pudding

One tablespoon sugar, 1½ tablespoon flour, 2 eggs, 1 teaspoon baking powder, flavoring. Beat well. Bake in quick oven 5 minutes; spread with jam, roll up, and pour a custard over.
— Mrs. F. Ingham.

Lemon Pudding

Stir into yolks of 6 eggs 1 cup sugar, ½ cup water and the grated rind and juice of 1 lemon. Soften 6 crackers or some slices of cake in warm water, lay in bottom of baking dish, pour custard over them and bake till firm. Beat whites until frothy, add 6 tablespoons sugar ; beat well. Pour over custard and brown. Eat warm or cold.
— Mrs. H. G. Tischer.

Lemon Cream

Three eggs, 2 tablespoons corn starch, 1 cup sugar, 1½ cups boiling water, 1 lemon. Have water boiling, add corn starch dissolved in a little cold water, sugar, juice and rind of lemon, beaten egg yolks, boil 5 minutes. Then stir in lightly the beaten egg white. Pour in glasses, put whipped cream on top.
— Mrs. J. W. Lane.

Lemon Pudding

Three cups milk, 1 cup sugar, 3 eggs, 2 tablespoons corn starch, 1½ lemon (juice and rind), pinch nutmeg, pinch salt. Cook starch in milk, when thick add beaten egg yolks, sugar, salt, nutmeg and lemon. Pour into a baking dish. Beat the whites with a little powdered sugar, put on top and bake a light brown. Can be served hot or cold.
— Mrs. J. W. Lane.

Mother's Surprise

Cover the bottom of a deep baking dish with thinly sliced buttered bread, spread with layer of strawberry preserves, another layer of buttered bread and preserves, and so on until desired amount is used. The last layer should be plain bread; add 1 cup milk and bake in hot oven 30 minutes. Uncover and brown. Serve with cream.
— Mrs. E. Ferch.

Orange Pudding

One-half cup sugar, 1 pint milk, 1 heaping tablespoon cornstarch, 2 eggs. Let sugar and milk come to a boil, add cornstarch, which has been dissolved in some of the milk. When done add eggs and 5 sliced oranges.
— Mrs. Louise M. Lafrentz.

Orange Pudding

Slice and sweeten 6 oranges, and ½ pound nuts. Place in layers alternately and put ½ pint of whipped cream flavored with maraschino on top.
— Mrs. Mandel Z.

Peaches Melba

Cut rounds of sponge cake or angel food and soften with a little sherry or fruit juice. Put a half peach on each round and fill with ice cream or whipped cream. Grate macaroons over all.
— Alicia K. Steinhoff.

Pineapple Whip

One-half pint whipping cream, 5 cents worth of marshmallows, 1 tablespoon sugar, 10 maraschino cherries, 5 slices of pineapple. Whip cream until stiff, add marshmallows, cut in small pieces, and let stand 1 hour. Just before serving add the fruit and sprinkle with chopped nuts when ready to serve.
— Mrs. G. C. Hass.

Pineapple Float

Mix 1 can shredded pineapple with ½ pint whipped cream, add sugar to taste and cut into it several marshmallows.
— Mrs. W. H. Jacobs.

Pineapple Dessert

Cut bread into rounds the size of a pineapple slice, dip into beaten egg and fry crisp in butter. Spread with orange marmalade, lay slice of pineapple on this and top with whipped cream.
— Ella Baerwald.

Prune Pudding

One-half pound prunes, 2 cups cold water, 1 cup sugar, 1⅓ cups boiling water, ⅓ cup corn starch, ½ teaspoon salt, 1 stick cinnamon. Wash and soak prunes, cook them in the 2 cups of water until soft. Cut in pieces, crack the stones and take out kernels and add to prunes. Add the boiling water and cinnamon, boil 5 minutes, take out the cinnamon, mix cornstarch with sugar and

salt and add to prunes ; boil until clear. Turn into a bowl that has been wet with cold water, chill and serve with cream.
— Miss Clara Wollerman.

Prune Whip

Stew 1 pound prunes with a little sugar and water until done, put through colander. Beat the whites of 2 eggs to a froth, mix with prunes, bake a few minutes. Serve with whipped cream.
— Mrs J. H. Kalte.

English Plum Pudding

One pound chopped beef suet, 1 pound currants, 1 pound large seedless raisins, 1 pound small raisins, 1 pound mixed lemon, orange and citron peel, 6 eggs, 1½ pounds brown sugar, 1 teaspoon ground cloves, 1 teaspoon ground allspice, 1 teaspoon ground cinnamon, 1 teaspoon ground nutmeg, i cup molasses, | cup tea mixed with molasses, 1 teaspoon salt, flour enough to mix all into a stiff batter, ½ cup whiskey, 2 cups milk, into which you have put ½ teaspoon soda. Boil for 6 hours.
— Mrs. W. R. Ahrens.

My Own Plum Pudding

One pound chopped suet, 1 pound each of brown sugar, currants, raisins, and breadcrumbs, 1 cup flour, 2 ounces mixed peel, pinch of salt, mixed spice to taste, a few chopped almonds and figs, 8 eggs, about ½ pint milk. Boil 3 hours. Makes 3 small puddings.
— Mrs. F. Ingham.

Thanksgiving Plum Pudding

Six crackers, 3 pints milk, ¼ cup butter, ½ teaspoon salt, 1 teaspoon mixed spices, 6 eggs, 1 pound seeded raisins. Soak crackers in milk. Cream butter and sugar, add salt, spices and eggs well beaten. Stir mixture into the milk, add raisins. Bake in a deep pudding dish well-buttered for 3 or 4 hours. Stir several times during the first hour to keep raisins from settling. Serve with or without hard sauce or whipped cream.
— Mrs. M. Eckhart.

Delicate Rice Pudding

Boil ½ cup rice in 1½ cups boiling water. When nearly done add 2 cups boiling milk and a pinch of salt. Cook until soft, then add ½ cup sugar and the well beaten yolks of 4 eggs. Beat in lightly the well beaten whites of 2 eggs and ½ teaspoon vanilla. Use the remaining whites for frosting. Put in oven and brown slightly.
— Mrs. M. Eckhart.

Raisin Pudding

Wash and dry 1 pound Sultana raisins, grease pudding dish. Put in a layer of boiled rice, over it a layer of raisins and continue until dish is nearly filled, having rice on top. Beat 2 eggs, add 2 teaspoons of sugar, pinch of salt, 2 tablespoons melted butter or butter substitute, and 2 cups sweet milk. Pour over pudding and bake 30 minutes. Serve with liquid sauce.
— Mrs. W. J. Keuer.

Snow Puff

To two cups of boiled rice add 1 cup of shredded pineapple and ½ pint whipped cream. Mix well and set in cool place until ready to serve. Sweeten to taste.

The success of this rule depends upon the cooking of the rice. Care should be taken that the rice is done and that the grains separate.
— H. E. Weisgerber.

Snow Pudding

Two cups water, 1 cup sugar, juice of 1 lemon, 2 egg whites, 2 heaping tablespoons corn starch. Boil sugar and water, thicken with corn starch dissolved in a little cold water; boil 4 minutes, then add lemon juice. Take from fire, beat into the stiffly beaten egg whites and continue beating for 10 minutes. Serve with custard or any preferred sauce, or with shredded pineapple and whipped cream.
— Alicia K. Steinhoff.

Strawberry Pudding

Take a quart of ripe berries and mash in a deep dish; sugar well. Scald 1 quart milk, add a pinch of grated lemon rind and thicken with cornstarch and the yolks of 2 eggs. Set aside to cool. Beat the 2 egg whites to stiff froth. Pour the custard over the berries, then the egg whites on top. Put in hot oven for few minutes to brown the egg whites slightly. Serve very cold.
— Flora Hemler.

STRAWBERRY PUDDING

One quart bread crumbs, 1 quart milk, 4 egg yolks, ½ cup sugar, ½ teaspoon salt, and a piece of butter the size of a walnut. Mix all together and bake. Spread with 3 pints sugared berries. Beat the egg whites with a little sugar, spread on the berries, and put in oven to brown.
— Mrs. Mandel Z.

STRAWBERRY AND RHUBARB SAUCE

One quart strawberries, 3 to 4 pounds rhubarb, sugar to taste. Procure crisp young rhubarb. Clean well with vegetable brush, trim off ends and cut into ½-inch lengths. Boil almost tender in a little water. Add the strawberries which have previously been cleaned and mashed, and sugar to taste. Boil until tender. Rasberries may be used in place of strawberries
— Johanna Kretchmer.

SUET PUDDING

One cup molasses, 1 cup milk, 1 cup chopped suet, a little salt, 3 cups flour, 2 cups raisins, 2 teaspoons soda, 1 teaspoon cinnamon, ½ teaspoon cloves. Steam 3 hours.
— Flora Hemler.

TAPIOCA CUSTARD

Put a pint of rich milk and 2 tablespoons of tapioca in a double boiler and cook slowly until transparent. Add the yolks of 2 eggs well-beaten and mixed with a pinch of salt and 3 tablespoons sugar. Stir and let cook slowly until thickened. When the custard is done add the stiffly beaten egg whites, take from fire and beat until cool; then add ½ teaspoon vanilla extract. If lump or pearl tapioca is used it should be soaked for several hours. If the top of this pudding is dotted with crabapple jelly it adds much to the appearance and flavor.
— Mrs. Mandel Z.

MOCK WHIPPED CREAM

A little powdered sugar added to the juice of 1 orange then to the stiffly beaten froth of 1 egg makes a good invalid dessert, also a good substitute for whipped cream.
— Mrs. O. Kleppisch.

Gelatine Desserts

Chocolate Bavarian Cream

Soak 1 box gelatine in 1 cup cold water 30 minutes. Whip 1 pint of cream and set on ice. Boil 1 pint of milk and add 2 ounces grated chocolate and the gelatine. When mixed take from stove and add ½ cup of sugar and vanilla to flavor. When cold add cream stirring carefully. Pour in mold and set on ice to harden.
— Mrs. R. Baur.

Maple Bavarian Cream

One cup maple syrup, ¼ package gelatine, 1 cup chopped walnuts, 1½ cups heavy cream, 3 eggs (separate yolks from whites) and ¼ cup cold water. Boil syrup and pour it gradually on the beaten eggs. Beat thoroughly and cook over hot water until thick. Add gelatine dissolved in cold water. Add nut meats. Set on ice until mixture begins to harden. Beat until frothy, fold in the whipped cream and whites of eggs and set away to harden.
— Mrs. R. Albrecht.

Cream Sponge

Soak 2 teaspoons of gelatine in cold water. Take juice of 1 orange and ½ lemon. Beat 2 eggs with ½ cup sugar, add this to the juice then the gelatine to which has been added less than ½ cup of boiling water; when just beginning to harden, add ½ pint of whipped cream. Add nuts and fruit and place some on top when cold.
— Mrs. R. Baur.

Grape-Nuts Fruit Pudding

One package lemon gelatine dissolved in 1 pint boiling water, 1 cup Grape-Nuts, ½ pound raisins or dates, as many walnuts as desired. Mix thoroughly and pour into a dish or mold to cool and harden. Serve with whipped cream.
— Mrs. H. A. Zom.

Gelatine Pudding

Two envelopes Knox Sparkling Gelatine, 7 eggs, 1 tablespoon vanilla, 1 quart milk, 1 cup sugar, 1 cup seedless raisins. Soak gelatine in 1 pint cold water ; add milk, sugar and raisins; heat, stirring until it comes to boiling point. Have yolks of eggs well beaten, add the hot milk, a little at a time so it will not curdle, but do not let it boil, then beat in the well beaten egg whites. Beat briskly until thoroughly mixed. Flavor and turn into mold. When ready to serve turn out on large flat dish and cover with whipped cream.
— Mrs. E. S. Berndt.

Lemon Sponge

Take the juice of 4 lemons, 4 eggs, 1 cupful of sugar, ½ package of gelatine, and 1 pint of water. Strain the lemon juice on the sugar, beat the yolks of the eggs and mix with the remainder of the water, having used half a cup of the pint in which to soak the gelatine, add the sugar and lemon to this and boil for about 1 minute, then remove from the fire and add the gelatine. Stir until the gelatine is dissolved, then strain into a dish and set in a cold place. When it begins to thicken, beat the whites of the eggs stiff and then pour the thickening gelatine gradually over the whites, beating continually until it is thoroughly mixed. Serve with whipped cream.
— Mrs. W. R. Ahrens.

Mock Ice Cream

Three tablespoons rice boiled in 1 pint milk, pinch salt, 1 tablespoon gelatine soaked in cold water. Whip ½ pint cream and add to first mixture.
— Mrs. C. B. Moellering.

Marchionesse Pudding

One pint whipping cream, 1 cup powdered sugar, ¼ box of Knox gelatine. Soak gelatine in cold water, then add hot water to dissolve, ¼ cup. Whip cream, add sugar, few drops vanilla, whites of 2 eggs, beaten stiff. When gelatine is cold, beat it into pudding and whatever fruit you want. Beat until it begins to thicken, then place in mold. If you wish it pink, use a few drops of food coloring. This serves ten people. Slice like ice cream and serve. — Mrs. R. Shotts.

Pineapple Pudding

One can grated pineapple, ⅔ cup sugar, 2 heaping teaspoons Knox gelatine, 1 cup boiling water, 1 cup whipped cream, juice of 1 lemon. Mix pineapple and sugar and boil until thick. Dissolve gelatine in boiling water and pour over pineapple. When cooled stir in the whipped cream and then add the lemon juice. — Mrs. H. Trippler.

Pineapple Pudding

Put 1 can of grated pineapple in saucepan, add 1 cup of sugar and 1 pint of water; boil until sugar is dissolved. Take 1 envelope of gelatine, dissolve in ½ cup of warm water and add pineapple. Let boil 3 minutes, pour in mold to cool. Serve with whipped cream. — Mrs. W. H. Mampe.

Pineapple Snow Pudding

Four eggs whites, beaten to a froth, 1 cup powdered sugar, ½ package gelatine, 1 cup lukewarm water, ½ can shredded pineapple. Gradually sift sugar into beaten whites. Dissolve gelatine in lukewarm water, and when dissolved add to whites. Then add pineapple. Beat about 10 minutes and set aside to stiffen.
MORE>

SAUCE. — Four egg yolks, 1 pint milk. Beat yolks to a froth. Put on milk to boil, then gradually add milk to yolks and a little sugar and vanilla to taste. Put on fire and just let come to boil. When ready to serve, pour over pudding.
— Johanna Kretchmer.

MOCK PLUM PUDDING

Into 1 package hot jello (any flavor) stir ¾ cup raisins, ¾ cup currants, ¾ cup stewed prunes, ¾ cup chopped nuts, ¾ cup Grape-Nuts, 1 teaspoon cinnamon, and ½ teaspoon ground cloves. Slice, when chilled, and serve with whipped cream.
— Mrs. E. H. Pierce.

RASPBERRY DELIGHT

Press 1 banana through a sieve add juice of ½ lemon, ½ cup of sugar, 1 egg well beaten. Beat all together until very light and set in a cold place. Dissolve 1 package of raspberry jello in 1 pint boiling water and turn into a mold to harden. When ready to serve, pour the banana mixture over.
— Mrs. Edw. J. Keuer.

RICE CREAM PUDDING

Soak 1 tablespoon gelatine 30 minutes, then add ¼ cup boiling water. Boil 5 tablespoons rice 30 minutes in plenty of water, then drain; when cold, add gelatine and 1 pint whipping cream, whipped stiff, to which has been added ¾ cup powdered sugar, 1 teaspoon vanilla and a pinch of salt, place on ice.
— Mrs. G. Leuthesser.

SPANISH CREAM

Beat the yolks of 4 eggs and 4 tablespoons sugar together until creamy. Cover half a box of gelatine with a little milk to dissolve it. Heat 4 cups milk to boiling point and add the dissolved gelatine, eggs and sugar and let it thicken but do not let it boil. Remove from fire, beat occasionally until perfectly cold, then add the stiffly beaten egg whites ; flavor with vanilla and cool on ice.
— Mrs. Mandel Z.

PIES

Pie Crust

One cup flour, 2 tablespoons lard or shortening, 2 tablespoons water. Cut and mix lard with flour, add water and roll.
— Mrs. H. Tripler.

Banana Cream Pie

Bake a very rich crust in deep pie tins, when done fill with 2 good size sliced bananas. **Filling:** ¾ cup sugar, 2 tablespoons flour, stir together. Butter the size of an egg, pinch of salt, yolks of 3 eggs, 1 pint of rich milk. Stir all together and cook in double boiler until thick. Remove from fire, flavor with 1 small teaspoon vanilla and pour over bananas. Beat whites of 3 eggs to a very stiff froth, add ¼ teaspoon cream of tartar, fold in 3 tablespoons of sugar, pile on top of cream and set in bottom oven to brown. This filling is enough for 2 pies.
— Mrs. Arthur Emde.

Butterscotch Pie
Boil 1 cup brown sugar, 2 tablespoons of flour, 1 cup water, 1 tablespoon butter, yolks of 2 eggs. Pour into a baked crust, put a meringue on top of pie and brown in a moderate oven.
— Mrs. H. W. Bruedigam.

Brown Sugar Pie

Cook until smooth ⅔ cup brown sugar, ½ tablespoon butter, 2 tablespoons milk. Mix together the yolks of 2 eggs, 2 heaping tablespoons flour and 2 cups milk. Add this to first mixture and boil till thick. Bake crust first and put a meringue on top of pie.
— Mrs. W. Brockschmidt.

Chocolate Pie
One cup sugar, ½ cup grated chocolate, 2 tablespoons cornstarch or flour, 2 cups boiling water, 2 eggs, 2 tablespoons butter, and 1 teaspoon vanilla. Blend together the sugar, chocolate and flour, add water and cook until thick. Then add the beaten yolks and let simmer for 5 minutes. Add the butter and vanilla and pour into a baked crust. Beat the whites stiff, add 3 tablespoons powdered sugar, place lightly over the top and brown.
— Mrs. Sodeman.

Cottage Cheese Pie

One cup fresh cottage cheese mashed fine, 2 well beaten eggs, ½ cup sugar and enough rich milk or cream to make the whole of the consistency of thin batter. Add a handful of currants and flavor with nutmeg or cinnamon. Pour over single crust as for custard pie and bake in moderate oven.
— Mrs. H. W. Bruedigam.

CRANBERRY PIE

One cup of cranberries, ½ cup raisins, 1 cup sugar, ½ cup hot water, 1 tablespoon vanilla, 1 tablespoon butter, 1 teaspoon flour mixed in with sugar. Mix all these ingredients together in a bowl. Line pie plate with crust, pour in the mixture, place top crust on and bake 20 minutes. This is delicious, and tastes like cherry pie.
— Mrs. R. Albrecht.

CREAM PIE

Two cups milk heated to scalding, ½ cup sugar mixed with 2 tablespoons flour, then add 1 tablespoon butter and well-beaten yolks of 2 eggs, any desired flavoring. Bake crust almost done, add custard. Beat whites of eggs, put on top and brown.
— Mrs. A. L. Dunfrund.

CUSTARD PIE

Beat well the yolks of 3 eggs. Stir thoroughly a tablespoon of sifted flour into 3 tablespoons of sugar; this separates the particles of flour so there will be no lumps. Add it to the yolks, put in a pinch of salt, a teaspoon full of vanilla and a little grated nutmeg; now add the beaten whites and lastly a pint of scalded, not boiled milk, which has been cooled. Mix this in by degrees and turn all into a deep pie tin lined with crust and bake 25 to 30 minutes.
— Mrs. Hunt.

Corn Custard Pie

One cup grated corn, ½ cup of milk, salt and cayenne to taste, butter the size of a walnut, 1 rounded tablespoon cornstarch, yolks of 2 eggs. Bake with an under crust only, and when done cover with a meringue made from the whites of 2 eggs, to which add a pinch of salt and a pinch of cream of tartar, but no sugar. Brown delicately.
— Mrs. Albrecht.

Lemon Cream Pie

Line a deep tin with a crust a little thicker than for fruit pies.

Filling. — Four tablespoons lemon juice, grated rind of 1 lemon, 1½ cups water, 1 cup sugar, ⅓ cup cornstarch, 3 egg yolks. Dissolve cornstarch in 4 tablespoons of water, put remainder of water, lemon juice and ½ the sugar into double boiler and let come to boiling point, then stir in the dissolved starch. Stir constantly until well thickened, then remove from direct heat, beat remaining sugar, lemon rind and yolks until creamy and stir into hot mixture. Pour into lined pie plate and bake in steady oven until well set. When done let cool before putting on meringue or it will draw moisture.

Meringue. — Beat 3 egg whites with pinch of salt until they froth, add ½ teaspoon cream of tartar and beat until stiff; add 3 tablespoons powdered sugar and 5 drops lemon extract. Pile on pie and brown in moderate oven. Let cool in warm place.
— Mrs. G. C. Hass.

Mapleine (Maple Extract) Pie

One cup milk, 3 level tablespoons corn starch, ¼ teaspoon salt, 2 tablespoons butter, J cup light brown sugar, 1 teaspoon Mapleine (maple extract). Heat milk in double boiler. Mix corn starch and salt perfectly smooth in ½ cup cold milk. Add to hot milk and cook until smooth and thick. Cook the butter and sugar until smooth and soft, and add to cornstarch mixture. Then add Mapleine (maple extract) and the two egg yolks beaten light and diluted with a little of the hot mixture. Cool slightly, fill baked pie shell, cover with meringue of remaining egg whites and brown slightly.
— Mrs. P. Weissbrodt.

Fruit Mincemeat

Two pounds of apples pared and cored, 1 pound raisins, 1 pound sultanas, 1 pound currants, ¾ pound beef suet, ½ pound stoned prunes, ½ pound figs, 4 ounces shelled almonds, juice and grated rind of 1 orange and 2 lemons, ¾ ounce of mixed ground spices, i pint cider. Mix thoroughly and put away in glass jars.
— Mrs. Albrecht.

Mincemeat

Three pounds of beef, ½ peck apples, 1 pound raisins, l pound currants, ½ pound suet, ½ pound citron, ½ gallon cider, 2 pounds brown sugar, 2 nutmegs grated, cinnamon and cloves to taste.
— Josephine O' Rourke.

Mincemeat

Four pounds beef, 2 pounds suet, 8 pounds apples, (pared and cored) 2 pounds currants, 2 pounds raisins, 1 pound citron, (may be omitted) 2 lemons, 2 oranges, 4 pounds brown sugar, ½ tablespoon mace, 1 tablespoon cinnamon, 1 tablespoon allspice, 2 tablespoons cloves, 2 tablespoons salt. Boil meat until tender, remove bones and put through food chopper. Chop suet and apples in small pieces, add oranges and lemons cut fine, and remaining ingredients. Mix with enough cider to scarcely cover. Cook 1 hour, and put in jars.
— Clare L. Kemnitz.

Pumpkin Pie

One cup strained pumpkin or squash, 1 cup cream or milk, 1 cup sugar, 3 eggs slightly beaten, ¼ cup cognac, ½ teaspoon nutmeg, 1 teaspoon ginger, 1 teaspoon cinnamon and salt.

Process. — Line a deep pan with rich paste. Wet the edges and lay a rim of pastry around 1 inch wide ; flute with the fingers and build rim up well. Wash over with the slightly beaten white of egg. Mix sugar and spices, add to squash or pumpkin, add eggs and cream slowly while beating briskly. Add brandy, fill crust and bake 35 minutes in a moderate oven.
— Mrs. Hunt.

Pumpkin Pie

Mix together 1¼ cups cooked and sifted pumpkin, 1 cup milk, ½ cup sugar, J teaspoon mace and 1 beaten egg. Bake about 40 minutes in a deep plate lined with pastry.
— Olga T. Bohnsack.

Mock Pumpkin Pie

One medium sized potato boiled and mashed, 1 heaping teaspoon butter, same of flour, 1 egg, ½ cup molasses, ½ cup sugar, and 1 cup of hot milk. Flavor with cinnamon, nutmeg and vanilla, and bake in one crust.
— Mrs. Anna Steging.

Sweet Potato Pie

One pound of steamed or boiled sweet potatoes finely mashed, 2 cups sugar, 1 cup cream, J cup butter, 3 well beaten eggs. Flavor with lemon or nutmeg and bake with an under crust.
— Alicia K. Steinhofif.

Squash Pie

Two cups boiled squash, 1 cup brown sugar, 3 eggs, 2 tablespoons molasses, 1 tablespoon melted butter, 1 tablespoon ginger, 1 teaspoon cinnamon, 2 cups sweet milk, pinch of salt.
— Mrs. Jacobs.

RAISIN PIE

One egg 1 lemon, 1 cup sugar, 1 tablespoon flour, 1 teaspoon cornstarch, ½ cup raisins. Cover raisins with 1 cup water and soak them for 2 hours. Beat the egg light with the sugar, add the strained lemon and the cornstarch ; then add the raisins and water, in which they were soaked. Cook until the mixture thickens. Cool and bake in 2 crusts.
— Mrs. R. J. Frank.

RHUBARB PIE

Pour boiling water over 2 cups chopped rhubarb. Drain off the water after 4 or 5 minutes and mix rhubarb with 1 cup sugar, 2 egg yolks, a piece of butter, 1 tablespoon flour, and moisten with 3 tablespoons water. Bake with lower crust only. Make a meringue of the whites of eggs, and 4 tablespoons sugar; spread over top of pie and return to oven to brown.
— Mrs. M. Brockman.

CHEESE AND EGGS

CHEESE BALLS

Put American cheese and stuffed olives through a meat grinder. Roll into balls and serve with crackers.
— Mrs. H. A. Zorn.

CHEESE FLUFF

Place cream cheese or a mild Neufchâtel in a bowl and pour on it thick sweet cream. With a fork whip to a fluffy mixture. Place cheese on lettuce hollow out a space in the center and fill with *bar-le-due* or currant jelly. — Alicia K. Steinhoff.

BAKED CRACKERS WITH CHEESE

Butter soda crackers, put on them as much grated cheese with a small speck of salt and pepper as each cracker will hold. Cook in hot oven till the cheese is melted, about 2 minutes. Serve at once.
— Alicia K. Steinhoff.

Cheese Soufflé

Put 2 tablespoons butter in a saucepan, add 2 tablespoons flour; when smooth add ¼ cup milk, salt, and a few grains cayenne. Cook 2 minutes ; add yolks of 2 eggs well beaten and ½ cup grated cheese. Let cool ; when cold add the whites beaten to a stiff froth. Turn into a buttered dish and bake 25 to 30 minutes. Serve at once.
— Alicia K. Steinhoff.

Welsh Rarebit

One cup milk, ¼ teaspoon cornstarch, 1 teaspoon butter, salt, cayenne, mustard. Stir until it thickens, add ½ pound American cheese when smooth. Serve on toast. — Mrs. H. G. Tischer.

Cheese Sandwiches

Take 20 cents worth of American cheese, 3 small cans pimentos, ½ pound boiled ham or ½ pound bacon fried, and put all through the food chopper. Mix with mayonnaise. This quantity is sufficient for about 50 sandwiches.
— Mrs. O' Rourke.

Cheese Sandwiches

One-half pound American cheese, 2 green peppers, 2 onions, 12 sweet pickles. Chop very fine and add mayonnaise dressing. Spread on buttered bread.
— Mrs. Graser.

Sandwich Filling

After removing the seeds of a sweet green pepper, chop fine and add to two cakes of Blue Label cheese. Thin all with mayonnaise dressing so it can be spread easily.
— Mrs. E. A. Bierdemann.

Cheese Straws

Roll plain pastry ¼ inch thick, sprinkle ½ with grated cheese (American) to which has been added a few grains of salt and cayenne. Fold, press edges firmly together, fold again, and roll out ¼ inch thick. Sprinkle with cheese and proceed as before. Repeat again. Cut in strips 6 inches long and ¼ inch wide. Bake 8 minutes in hot oven. Pile log cabin fashion and serve with salad.
— Mrs. F. Nyendorf.

Bird's Nest Toast

Toast bread a light brown. Beat the white of 1 egg, put on top of a piece of toast and put yolk in center; put in oven to brown.
— Mrs. Sodeman.

Egg Cutlets

Blend 1 tablespoon flour with 1 tablespoon butter. Add ½ cup hot milk and cook thick. Add 3 or 4 hard boiled eggs, chopped fine, salt, pepper, a pinch of onion and parsley. Make into balls and fry in hot lard.
— Mrs. Pl. G. Tischer.

Escalloped Eggs

Place 6 eggs in boiling water and keep the eggs simmering for 30 minutes. Then lay eggs in cold water for 5 minutes. Remove shells, cut whites in thin slices, place in a baking dish and crumble the yolks over them. Make a white sauce of 2 tablespoons butter, 2 tablespoons flour, and 1 pint milk; season with salt and pepper. Pour over the prepared eggs and spread 1 cup of buttered crumbs on top. Bake about 15 minutes in a hot oven.
— Alicia K. Steinhoff.

Deviled Eggs

Peel and cut in half 12 hard boiled eggs. Take out the yolks and mash smooth while warm. Mix 1 heaping teaspoon butter, 1 level teaspoon mustard, 2 tablespoons vinegar, and 1 heaping teaspoon sugar. Mix with yolks and put back in the whites. Put a thin slice of sweet green or red pepper on top.
Very good.
— Mrs. Sodemann.

Stuffed Eggs

Cut hard boiled eggs into halves. Rub yolks to a cream with melted butter; add minced ham, salt, pepper and a little mustard. Fill the whites with this mixture : Tongue, minced olives, minced mushrooms or capers may be used instead of ham.
— Mrs. H. A. Zorn.

Omelet with Chicken Livers

Scald 3 chicken livers, drain cover with fresh boiling water and simmer for 20 minutes. Drain and cut in tiny cubes. Put in a frying pan with 1 heaping teaspoon butter, 10 drops onion juice, and 1 tablespoon finely chopped mushrooms. Shake and turn until well colored. Beat 6 eggs slightly, add 3 tablespoons water, ¼ teaspoon salt and a dash of pepper. Melt 1 teaspoon butter in a frying pan, and when hot, turn in the beaten eggs. When set, spread the prepared livers in the center of the omelet, fold, turn out on a hot platter and serve at once.
— Mrs. R. Albrecht.

Omelet with Fried Tomatoes

Wipe and peel 2 tomatoes; cut in two slices; three if large. Sprinkle with salt and pepper and dredge with flour. Fry 1 teaspoon onion in 1 tablespoon butter, till yellow ; draw it to one side and quickly fry the tomatoes, adding more butter if needed. Place on a hot platter and then make a plain omelet with 2 to 4 eggs, according to size desired. Beat the eggs slightly with a fork, add a dash of pepper and 1 tablespoon hot water to each egg. Turn into hot buttered frying pan, and as it thickens draw the cooked part to the center; when nearly all thick shake on a little salt. Let it color slightly, turn out on platter having the tomatoes arranged around it.
— Mrs. H. G. Tischer.

Scrambled Eggs with Tomato

Melt 2 tablespoons butter, add 1 tablespoon each of chopped green pepper and onion, 1 cup cooked tomato, ½ teaspoon salt. When hot, add 4 eggs slightly beaten; stir carefully, and when scrambled serve on toast.
— Alicia K. Steinhoff.

DUMPLINGS AND NOODLES

NEVER FAIL DUMPLINGS

One and one-half cups flour, 1 teaspoon baking powder, pinch salt. Mix, add 1 egg and f cup sweet milk. Stir and drop by the spoonful into boiling chicken, veal, or lamb broth. Keep covered for 5 minutes, then uncover and boil a few minutes longer. Serve at once.
— Mrs. A. J. Koehneke.

STEAMED DUMPLINGS

Two cups flour, 2 teaspoons baking powder, 2 eggs, ½ teaspoon salt, 7 tablespoons milk. Mix well and drop in steamer with tablespoon. Nice with stewed chicken.
— Mrs. Sodemann.

CORN DUMPLINGS

Make a nice light biscuit dough and form it into small, thin rounds, just large enough to hold 1 heaping tablespoon corn, seasoned to taste. Add a lump of butter and form into round dumplings. Steam for about 30 minutes and serve as a garnish for stewed chicken.
— Mrs. Albrecht.

Cracker Dumplings

One heaping tablespoon butter, 3 eggs, 10 crackers, nutmeg and lemon rind to taste. Stir butter to cream, add yolks of eggs, nutmeg and lemon rind; add whites of eggs, beaten stiff, and lastly crackers, rolled fine. Form little balls, drop in boiling soup and let boil for a few minutes.
— Mrs. John C. Koebel.

Farina Dumplings

Boil ¼ cup farina in 1 cup soup, then remove from stove add 1 egg and nutmeg to taste. Drop into soup from a tablespoon and boil 5 minutes before serving.
— Mrs. Wm. Bohnsack.

Liver Dumplings

One pound calf's liver, 2 eggs, 3 slices white bread, 1¼ cups flour. Chop liver fine, add beaten eggs and bread. Allow to stand until bread is soft, then add flour, pepper and salt. Drop into boiling broth and boil about 20 minutes.
— Mrs. Wm. Hinrichs.

Meat Dumplings (for Soup)

One-half pound chopped beef and pork, 2 slices stale white bread (soaked in cold water and pressed dry), 1 egg, 1 good-sized grated onion, parsley, pepper, salt, nutmeg to taste. Mix all together, form in small balls. Boil in soup 10 minutes without a cover.
— Mrs. C. B. Moellering.

Potato Dumplings

Grate 6 boiled potatoes and add 4 or 5 rolled crackers, then add 2 eggs beaten with 1 spoon milk. Mix, add 1 teaspoon salt, pinch of baking powder and enough flour to handle. Form into balls and drop into boiling water; cook 30 minutes.
— Mrs. Mandel Z.

Potato Dumplings

Boil and mash about 10 medium sized potatoes, or use left over potatoes and grate them. Then grate about 20 raw potatoes and squeeze dry in cheese cloth. Mix all together and add about 3 slices white bread cut into cubes, shape into balls, put into boiling water and boil 30 minutes. Serve with pork roast or Sauerbraten.
— Mrs. Wm. C. Hinricks.

FILLED NOODLES

This recipe will make enough for 4 or 5 persons. Cook ½ peck spinach well, drain and chop real fine. Fry 1½ pounds pork shoulder and when done put through meat chopper so it will be real fine; season with pepper, salt, a little nutmeg and 2 eggs. Mix with the gravy from the fried pork. Make noodle dough and roll out; they should not be too dry, cut them in triangles or 3-inch three cornered pieces. Put about 1 tablespoon filling on each and roll up. Wet edge and close all around. Cook them in salt water, drain in colander; when cold fry in butter.
— Mrs. E. S. Berndt.

FILLED NOODLES

Make a regular noodle dough with 4 eggs ; do not roll too thin, and do not allow them to dry. Cut into 7-inch squares, and put on each one a large tablespoon of the following mixture: 1 pound chopped beef, veal or pork, together or separately (leftovers are good for this), add ½ pound of bread or crackers soaked in water and squeezed out, 4 eggs, salt and pepper, finely chopped onion. Mix all ingredients well, fill the squares and then fold over the ends to the center like an envelope and pat them about f inch thick. Put in boiling salt water and boil 20 minutes. Strain and serve with butter and gravy, or use in soup.
— Mrs. Mandel Z.

Potato Noodles

Boil 8 potatoes and put through ricer on bread board, make hollow in center and add 2 cups flour, 3 beaten eggs, 1 teaspoon salt; knead it, cut in strips, roll with hands and cut into little pieces. Roll each into inch length and thickness of a pencil; boil about 5 minutes in 4 quarts boiling water and 1 tablespoon salt. Strain and pour over some melted butter. Serve with browned bread or cracker crumbs.
— Ada Burhop Bohnsack.

Erste Deutsche Evangelische Kirche in Elmira, New York built in 1899 is now known as First United Church of Christ. This church is in the National Register of Historic Places.

FRITTERS, DOUGHNUTS PANCAKES

Apple Fritters

Two cups flour, 2 tablespoons sugar, ¼ teaspoon salt, 1 cup milk, 1 egg, 4 teaspoons baking powder. Mix and sift dry ingredients, add beaten egg to milk add tablespoon melted lard. Pare the apples cut in small pieces, and mix in batter, drop by spoonful into hot lard and fry until brown.
— Mrs. F. Nyendorf.

Apple Fritters

Pass through a sieve, 1 cup flour, 1 level teaspoonful baking powder, 1 level tablespoonful powdered sugar, and ¼ teaspoonful salt. Beat 1 egg until very light; add ¼ cup of milk, and stir it in to the dry ingredients. Then stir in two apples, pared, cored and cut in small bits. Have ready a kettle of hot fat ; drop the batter into the fat by spoonfuls and let fry until delicately browned. Drain on soft paper, serve with powdered sugar or a jelly sauce. Bananas, peaches, (fresh fruits or canned) may be used.
— Mrs. Anna A. Jaekel.

Banana Fritters

Mix 1 cup flour, 1 teaspoon baking powder, 2 tablespoons sugar, ¼ teaspoon of salt. Beat 1 egg light with ⅓ cup of milk, then add to dry ingredients. Then add 3 fine mashed bananas, and 1 tablespoon of lemon juice. Drop by the spoonful in deep fat and fry. Drain on paper and sprinkle with powdered sugar.
— Mrs. W. C. Henrichs.

Doughnuts

One cup sugar, 1½ cups milk, 1½ pints flour, 1 tablespoon butter or lard, 1 egg, 2 teaspoons baking powder, ½ teaspoon salt, a little nutmeg. Mix into a soft dough. Flour board well ; roll out dough to the thickness of one-half inch, cut and fry a light brown in plenty of hot lard. Sift powdered sugar over.
— Mrs. Carrie Smith.

Snow Ball Doughnuts

One cup sugar, creamed with 4 level teaspoons of melted butter. Add 2 well beaten eggs, 1 cup sweet milk, 1 teaspoon grated nutmeg, flour to admit handling, and 2 rounded teaspoons baking powder, sifted well with flour. Roll to 1-inch thick, fry in lard a gold brown. Makes 3 dozen.
— Mrs. G. Massman.

Buttermilk Doughnuts

One cup sugar (heaping) ½ teaspoon salt, 1 tablespoon melted butter, 3 eggs, nutmeg (enough to flavor), 1 teaspoon of baking

soda dissolved in 1 cup butter milk. Add enough flour to be able to roll. (Do not get it too stiff.) Roll about ¼ inch thick, cut and fry in deep hot fat. Dust with powdered sugar.
— Clara L. Kemnitz.

Potato Doughnuts

One cup mashed potatoes, 1 cup sugar, 3 eggs, 1 tablespoon butter, 1 teaspoon vanilla, 1 teaspoon lemon extract, ½ teaspoon salt, 2 teaspoons baking powder, 1 cup milk, and flour to make a soft dough.
— Mrs. R. J. Frank.

Bread Crumb Pancakes

One pint sour milk, 1 cup bread crumbs, 2 eggs beaten, 1 tablespoon sugar, little salt, and flour enough to make the dough not too stiff. Just before baking add a scant teaspoon soda dissolved in a little hot water.
— Marie Doederlein.

Cornmeal Pancakes

Two beaten eggs and beat into them a little sugar and a pinch of salt, add 2 cups milk, 1½ cups flour and 1½ cups cornmeal and 3 teaspoons baking powder. Sift the dry ingredients well together. These are light and spongy.
— Mrs. H. W. Bruedigam.

Egg Pancakes

Four eggs well beaten, 1½ cups flour, 1 pint milk, 1 teasspoon salt. Butter must be perfectly smooth like a heavy cream. Just before turning place a tiny bit of fat in center of pancake. Makes about 6 large pancakes.
— Mrs. J. Semmlow.

Potato Pancakes

Peel and grate some raw potatoes, put in a coarse cloth and squeeze out as much of the water as possible. To one pint of the dry potatoes add 4 eggs, well beaten, 4 tablespoons of thick, sour cream, ½ teaspoon salt, and 2 tablespoons flour. Have ½-inch of fat in frying pan and when smoking hot drop a spoonful of the mixture. When brown on one side turn and brown quickly on the other, and serve at once.
— Mrs. R. Albrecht.

Potato Pancakes

Grate 10 good sized potatoes into a pan with cold water. When all are grated drain in a fine sieve or lay a piece of cheesecloth on a colander and press out all the water. To the pulp add 4 eggs and 1 teaspoon salt. Have the griddle very hot and well greased. Put in 2 tablespoons of batter and spread out into a flat cake. Bake to a crisp brown on both sides. Do not use the least bit of flour or they will be spoiled.
—Mrs. O. A. Skibbe.

Strawberry Pancakes

Beat the yolks of 2 eggs and add a batter made of 1 cup flour, into which has been stirred 1 teaspoon baking powder, a large pinch salt, 1 cup milk and 1 teaspoon butter, melted. Beat all together, add 1 cup strawberries cut in halves and dredged with flour. Just before beginning to bake cakes fold in the stiffly beaten egg whites. Bake on a well greased griddle and serve with butter and powdered sugar.
— Mrs. F. Schoenwolf.

Waffles

Beat 3 eggs well; mix thoroughly 4 cups flour with 3 teaspoons baking powder, add ½ cup butter to this; add the eggs and enough milk to make a thin batter which will pour easily.
— Miss L. Gansz.

Waffles

One pint of sour milk 3 tablespoons melted butter, 3 eggs beaten separately, 1 teaspoon soda dissolved in a little warm water; add a little salt and stir in enough flour to make a stiff batter. Bake upon waffle irons.
— Mrs. Albrecht.

First Evangelical Lutheran Church. This church is in the National Register of Historic Places. It was founded in 1850 in Galveston by German immigrants as First German Evangelical Lutheran Church.

BAKING POWDER BREADS AND COFFEE CAKES

Baking Powder Biscuits

Four cups flour, 1 teaspoon salt, 4 teaspoons baking powder, 1 tablespoon each of butter and lard, 2 cups milk. Sift the dry ingredients; cut and rub the butter and lard into the mixture; add milk gradually. Turn on well floured board, roll lightly to 1 inch thick, cut with biscuit cutter and bake in a hot oven from 15 to 20 minutes.
— Mrs. Graser.

Bran Bread

Two cups bran, 1 cup white flour, 1½ cups buttermilk, ½ cup sugar, 1 teaspoon salt, 1 heaping teaspoon soda, 1 heaping teaspoon baking powder. Mix bran, flour, sugar, salt and baking powder together well. Add soda to buttermilk and then to mixture. Place in greased pans. Let rise 30 minute and bake 1 hour. This makes 2 loaves.
— Mrs. R. Shotts.

Brown Bread

Two and one-half cups of sour milk, ¾ cups of molasses, 1 teaspoon salt, 2 teaspoons soda in 1 cup white flour, 2 cups bran, 2 cups graham flour. If you haven't both, 4 cups of either kind of flour will do and 1 cup raisins. Bake about an hour in covered tins. I use baking powder cans and only fill them half full. They raise so much.
— Mrs. G. H. Rausch.

Brown Bread

One cup brown sugar 1 teaspoon butter, 1 egg, 1 teaspoon salt, 1 teaspoon soda, 4 cups graham flour, enough sour milk to make a rather stiff batter. Bake slowly from ¾ to 1 hour.
— Mrs. H. Tischer.

Boston Brown Bread

One cup yellow meal, ½ cup rye meal, ½ cup graham flour, ½ cup wheat flour, 1 cup milk, ½ cup molasses, ¼ teaspoon salt. Mix well together, pour into greased brown bread mold. Steam 3 hours; dry off 10 minutes in oven. If sour milk is used, use 1 teaspoon soda in milk. If sweet milk is used add 1½ teaspoons baking powder.
— Mrs. H. Kaeppel.

Cinnamon Rolls

Two cups flour, 4 teaspoons baking powder, 4 tablespoons butter, ¾ cup milk, pinch of salt, ½ cup sugar. Cut butter into the dry ingredients and add milk, a little at a time. Roll the dough out to about ½ inch and spread 2 tablespoons melted butter over. Sprinkle 2 tablespoons sugar and 1 teaspoon, cinnamon with ½ cup of raisins over top. Roll up in jelly roll fashion and cut into 1 inch pieces. Place close together in greased tin and bake 15 to 20 minutes in moderate oven.
— Mrs. E. J. Keuer.

Apple Coffee Cake

One large cup flour, 2 teaspoons baking powder, ¼ teaspoon salt, ½ cup sugar, 3 tablespoons shortening, lard and butter. Put 1 egg in cup, beat, and fill with milk. Mix all well together. Flour hands and spread in baking pan; cover top with apples and sugar and little cinnamon; put bits of butter on if you like. Bake about 20 minutes. This is very good.
— Mrs. Klipp.

Coffee Cake

One-half cup butter, 1 cup sugar, 1 cup milk, 2 eggs, 2 cups flour, 2 teaspoons baking powder, put in coffee cake tins, then strew over the top, well mixed, ¼ cup grated bread-crumbs, ¼ cup sugar, 1 teaspoon cinnamon, over this put ¼ cup melted butter.
— Mrs. W. H. Bruedigam.

OMA KUEHL'S TEA CAKE

Twelve eggs beaten, 2 cups flour, 4 cups milk, 1 teaspoon sugar, ¼ teaspoon salt. Grease bread tins, fill 1½ inch. Bake in quick oven, will raise to top of pan, when done spread butter and sugar on top and serve at once.
— Mrs. Semmlow.

CRUMB CAKE

Two cups flour, 1½ cups sugar, | cup butter, 2 teaspoons baking powder. Mix with the hands until flaky then set aside ½ cup of this mixture. Yolks of 2 eggs well beaten, mix with ¾ cups milk; add this to the first mixture, then add the stiffly beaten whites of eggs, 1 teaspoon vanilla. Mix well and put in tins ; add 1 teaspoon cinnamon to the ½ cup crumbs; spread on top of cake. Bake in slow oven about 30 minutes.
— Mrs. H. Schoenwolf.

DELICIOUS CORN BREAD

Two cups cornmeal, 1 quart milk, 4 eggs, 1 tablespoon melted butter, 1 teaspoon salt, 1 teaspoon sugar. Beat the eggs thoroughly, add the meal, butter, salt and sugar and when well mixed, the milk which has been put over the fire to scald. Pour into a buttered pan and put at once into the oven. The batter is very thin but needs no more meal as the eggs will stiffen sufficiently.
— Mrs. Albrecht.

Cream Cornmeal Puffs

Mix well together 1½ cups cornmeal, 1½ cups flour, 2 tablespoons sugar and 1 teaspoon salt. Beat the yolks of 2 eggs, add 1½ cups cream and ^ cup milk and stir into the dry mixture. Beat well, stir in the stiffly whipped whites of the eggs and 2 teaspoons baking powder and bake in well-greased gem pans in a hot oven.
— Mrs. Albrecht.

Cornmeal Muffins
One-half cup butter, ½ cup sugar, 1 cup milk, 2 eggs, pinch of salt, 1 cup of cornmeal (white), 1 cup flour. Add little more flour to batter, not too stiff, like cake batter. One and one-half heaping teaspoons baking powder. Bake in buttered gem pans in moderate oven.
— Mrs. H. G. Thoms.

Gingerbread

One cup molasses, ½ cup sugar, 1 cup sour cream (sour milk will do), 1 egg, 2½ cups flour, 1 teaspoon ginger, ½ teaspoon nutmeg, 1 rounding teaspoon soda.
— Josephine O'-Rourke.

Gingerbread
One cup sour milk, 1 cup shortening, 1 cup molasses, 2 eggs, 1½ cups sugar, 4 cups flour, 2 teaspoons soda, 2 teaspoons cinnamon, ½ teaspoon cloves, 1 tablespoon ginger. Bake slowly in dripping pan at least 40 minutes. Add no more flour.
— Mrs. Edw. H. Pierce.

Graham Bread

Two cups sour milk, 2 eggs, ½ cup molasses, 2 level teaspoons soda, pinch salt, 1 cup white flour and enough graham to make a stiff batter. Small teaspoon baking powder in the white flour. Bake 1 hour.
— Mrs. E. Pierce.

Graham Nut Bread

Two cups white flour 2 cups graham flour, 4 teaspoons baking powder, 1 teaspoon salt, 1 cup sugar. Sift together and add 2 eggs, 2 cups milk, 1 cup walnuts (cut not too fine, rather medium). Beat well and put in buttered pans. Let raise 20 minutes and bake in moderate oven.
— Mrs. H. Berger.

Kugelhupf

Three eggs, 1 scant cup sugar, 1 large tablespoon butter, 1 scant cup currants (floured), 3 cups of flour, 1 teaspoon salt, 1½ cups of milk, 2 heaping teaspoon of baking powder. Put into form pan. Bake 45 minutes in moderate oven.
— Mrs. R. Baur.

Tea Muffins

Work butter size of an egg into 2 cups flour, add ½ teaspoon salt, 2 tablespoon sugar, 2 even teaspoons baking powder and stir together thoroughly. Beat 1 egg, add to it 1 cup of milk, mix it with the flour quickly, and bake in a hot oven.
— Mrs. R. Baur.

Twin Mountain Muffins

Cream ⅓ cup butter, add gradually ¼ cup sugar and ¼ teaspoon salt; add 1 egg beaten light, ¾ cup milk, 2 cups sifted flour and 4 level teaspoons baking powder. Bake in hot buttered gem pans about 20 minutes.
— Marie Doederlein.

Nut Bread

One cup brown sugar, 2 cups sweet milk, 1 cup chopped nuts, 4 cups flour, 1 teaspoon salt, 4 teaspoons baking powder, 2 eggs. Mix and let stand in pans 20 minutes, then bake 1 hour in slow oven.
— Mrs. Wm. Fredericks.

Nut Bread

One cup chopped walnuts or hickory nuts, 4 cups flour mixed with 4 teaspoons baking powder, 1 tablespoon salt, 2 tablespoons sugar, 2 cups milk, 1 egg beaten light. Let rise 1 hour. Bake in 1 loaf for 1 hour.
— Mrs. O. Kleppisch.

Whole Wheat Nut Bread

One egg, ½ cup sugar, ½ teaspoon salt, ½ cups sweet milk, 1 cup chopped walnuts, 2 cups whole wheat flour, 1½ cups white flour, and 3 teaspoons baking powder. Mix and allow to rise 20 minutes, then bake in a moderate oven for 45 minutes.
— Mrs. A. J. Koehneke.

Pop-Overs

Two eggs, 1 cup flour, 1 cup milk, 1 teaspoon salt. Beat hard, and bake 35 minutes in moderate oven.
— Helen Lindau.

Blueberry Shortcake

Make a baking powder coffee cake dough. Place in a long pan bringing dough up on sides of pan. Mix 1 egg beaten light, ½ cup milk, sugar to taste with 1 quart of blue or huckleberries. Pour mixture on dough. Quick oven.
— Mrs. J. Semmlow.

Sauce for Orange Shortcake

Peel oranges, remove white skin and slice as thinly as possible. Put 1 cup sugar, ½ cup water and orange juice in a saucepan and let boil a little. Pour this syrup over a well beaten egg; beat as for cake frosting. Cover cake with sliced oranges and pour sauce over.
— Mrs. Semmlow.

YEAST BREADS

Graham Bread

Four cups graham flour, 3½ cups flour, 2 tablespoons molasses, 3 cups lukewarm milk, 1 cake yeast, 1 heaping teaspoon salt, 2 tablespoons brown sugar, ½ teaspoon soda, 2 tablespoons butter, ½ cup lukewarm water. Sift together the graham flour, wheat flour, brown sugar and salt, then rub in the butter. Add the molasses with the soda dissolved in it. Next add the lukewarm milk and lastly the yeast dissolved in the lukewarm water. Knead the dough well for 20 minutes and set it to rise covered up. After rising form it into two loaves, put them into pans and let them rise again. Graham bread requires longer to rise than white flour bread. Bake in a moderately hot oven for an hour and a quarter. If graham bread is baked too quickly it is apt to become doughy in the center. The above makes two loaves of bread.
— Mrs. Ehlenfeld.

Quaker Oats Bread

Two cups quaker oats, 5 cups flour, 2 cups boiling water, 1 cake yeast, ½ cup molasses, ½ tablespoon butter, small handful salt. Add boiling water to oats and allow to stand one hour. Add molasses, salt, butter, dissolved yeast and flour; let rise until double in bulk, beat thoroughly, turn into buttered pans, let rise again. Bake one hour in two loaves.
— Mrs. O. Kleppisch.

Swedish Rye Bread

Heat 1 pint milk and 1 pint water to boiling point, add 1 tablespoon lard, 1 tablespoon butter, ½ cup brown sugar, ½ cup corn syrup, 1 tablespoon salt, 1 tablespoon caraway seed, 1 tablespoon anise seed. Beat in 2 quarts rye flour (beat hard). Dissolve 1| cake yeast in a little warm water and add to above when lukewarm, add enough white flour so you can knead, about 20 minutes. Let rise and knead again. Shape into loaves and brush top with egg white or butter. Bake in hot oven for 15 minutes, then decrease heat and bake until done.
— Mrs. P. Weissbrodt.

White Bread

Put 1 quart lukewarm milk or water in bread mixer, add 2 teaspoons salt, 2 tablespoons sugar, 2 tablespoons shortening, 1 packet yeast which has been dissolved in ½ cup lukewarm water, and 3 quarts flour. Turn bread mixer about 5 minutes, let rise over night and form in loaves in the morning, when raised again bake 45 minutes. Have oven hot for 10 minutes, then turn gas down to medium.
— Olga T. Bohnsack.

Nut Bread

One-half cup water, 1½ cups milk, 1 yeast cake softened in 1 cup water, 4 tablespoons molasses, 1 teaspoon salt, ½ pound filbert meats, 4 cups entire wheat flour, 2 cups sifted white flour. Add

the softened yeast cake to lukewarm milk and water, molasses, salt and nuts, and stir in the flour. A little more flour may be required. Knead the dough until elastic, then set to rise. When light, shape in loaves and when again light bake about 1 hour.
— Olga T. Bohnsack.

French Rolls

Scald 1 pint of milk, dissolve in it 1 tablespoon butter, 1 teaspoon sugar and ½ teaspoon salt; when lukewarm add ½ of a yeast cake dissolved in 2 tablespoons of warm water and sufficient sifted bread flour to make a batter. Beat until smooth and set aside, covered in a warm place until light. Add more flour to make a soft dough, turn out on the board and knead until smooth and springy to the touch. Return to the bowl, cover and set away again until light. Take out portions of the dough about the size of a large egg and roll each out until as thick as the middle finger, then form into crescents or other, desired shapes ; or all the dough may be turned out carefully on the board and rolled out an inch thick, then cut with cutters of various shapes. Lay an inch apart on greased pans, brush the top of each roll with milk and when light bake in a very hot oven.
— Mrs. Albrecht.

Parker House Rolls

Two cups scalded milk, ½ cup lukewarm water, 1 cake yeast, ½ cup melted butter, 1 teaspoon salt, 2 tablespoons sugar. Mix yeast with water; when milk is lukewarm add the yeast; to it add

enough flour to make a thin batter ; let rise until light ; add sugar, salt, melted butter, flour enough to make a soft dough ; knead for 20 minutes; let rise until doubled in bulk. Roll out I inch thick, cut with a biscuit cutter; press the handle of a wooden spoon across the center of each, making a crease, butter ½ slightly; fold the other half over on it; set in a pan some distance apart ; let rise until light and bake from 18 to 20 minutes.
— Miss Clara Wollerman.

Tea Biscuits

One cup scalded milk, 1 tablespoon sugar, 2 tablespoons shortening, ½ teaspoon salt, 1 yeast cake dissolved in ½ cup water, 4 cups flour. Put the sugar, salt, and shortening in a mixing bowl; add scalded milk, when lukewarm; add yeast cake and 3 cups flour slowly. Beat to a light batter. Let rise to double its bulk, then add 1 cup flour; let rise again. Shape in biscuits form ; let rise till light and bake in quick oven 25 minutes.
— Mrs. Sodemann.

Cinnamon Buns

Scald 1 pint of milk, dissolve in it 1 scant teaspoon salt, 1 tablespoon butter and 2 tablespoons sugar. When cool add ½ of a cake of yeast, dissolved in a little warm water, and sufficient flour to make a drop batter. Cover and set aside until light, add flour to make a soft dough and knead for 5 minutes. Return to the bowl, cover and set aside as before. When light turn out carefully on the well floured board and roll out i of an inch thick. Spread with

softened butter, sprinkle with granulated sugar, cleaned currants and a little powdered cinnamon. Roll up tightly and cut in 2-inch slices. Put close together in well greased pans and when light bake in a moderate oven from 40 to 50 minutes. Turn out as soon as taken from the oven or they will stick. The excellence of these buns depends upon the amount of butter and sugar used when spread, the more the better.
— Mrs. Albrecht.

Coffee Cake

One quart flour, 2 cups milk, ½ cup butter and lard, ½ cup sugar, 2 eggs, 1 cent yeast, salt. Add little salt to flour, dissolve yeast in a little of the milk slightly warmed, heat remainder of milk slightly, adding butter and lard. Mix milk, butter, lard with flour; add eggs and sugar and beat. Let rise until light. Put in pans, spread with melted butter, sugar and cinnamon. Let rise again and bake.
— Mrs. L. C. Koebel.

Form Cake or Kugelhupf

Three cups flour, 1 cup milk, ⅔ cup sugar, ½ pound butter, 7 eggs, 1 packet yeast, ½ teaspoon salt, ¼ lemon peel (grated). Stir half of the flour with the yeast and milk. Cream the butter and add alternately eggs and flour. Also sugar, lemon and salt. Then stir the first part to it thoroughly, place in a buttered form and allow to rise. Bake 1 hour in a moderate oven.
— Mrs. C. B. Moellering.

German Napfkuchen

Three and one-half cups flour (sifted), 1 packet yeast, 1 cup warm milk, ¾ cup granulated sugar, ½ pound butter, 5 eggs, 1 cup blanched and finely ground almonds, 1 cup seedless raisins, 1 pinch mace, ½ lemon rind (grated), ½ juice of lemon. Set sponge with the milk, yeast and 1½ cups flour. When light, cream the butter and sugar, add the well beaten eggs with yolks and mix gradually with the risen sponge, which has been beaten until bubbles appear (about 20 minutes). Pour in a well-greased spring tube form and set to rise until about one inch from top of form. Bake in moderate oven about 1 hour.
—Mrs. H. G. Thorns.

Stollen

Heat 1 quart of milk, 1¼ cup sugar and 1¼ cup butter. When this is cool, add 3 quarts flour, 1 teaspoon salt. 2 cakes yeast, 3 beaten eggs, 6 oz. citron (cut fine), 1 pound light seedless raisins, 1 pound grated almonds, juice of ½ lemon and the rind of 1 lemon. Let this rise as you would bread, put in 4 bread pans, making in loaf forms, and when in pans let it rise again. Bake 30 minutes. Frost as you would angel cake.
— Mrs. Albrecht.

Stollen or Raisin Bread

Four pounds flour, 1 quart milk, 4 eggs, 2½ ounces yeast, 1¼ pounds butter, 1 pound Sultana raisins, 1 ½ pounds sugar, ¼ pound chopped almonds, 6 ounces citron (chopped). In the morning make a sponge from part of the flour, add the lukewarm milk, beaten eggs, yeast and salt. Set in warm place to rise. It will rise very quickly. Then add softened butter, raisins, sugar, almonds, citron (flour the almonds, raisins and citron), and the balance of flour. Grate a little lemon rind into dough. Now let rise again, then mold into loaves and raise once more, when they are ready for the oven. Spread melted butter before putting in oven, and bake slowly for 1 hour or longer. Have every ingredient warm before you begin mixing.
— Marie Doederlein.

Main building of the German United Evangelical Church Complex in Rochester, New York.

COOKIES

ANISE SEED COOKIES

Rub to a cream ½ cup butter and 1 cup powdered sugar. When light, stir in the well beaten yolks of 3 eggs then add the stiffened whites alternately with a pound of flour or enough to make a stiff dough, first stirring into the flour 1 teaspoonful of anise seed. Roll thin, cut into rounds and bake.
— Mrs. Chas. Hemler.

BREAD CRUMB COOKIES

One cup granulated sugar, ½ cup shortening butter or lard, 1 egg, 1 teaspoon baking soda mixed in ½ cup sour milk or ½ cup hot water, 1/2 cup bread crumbs, 1½ cup flour, ½ teaspoon salt, 2 teaspoon cinnamon, ½ teaspoon baking powder. Drop cookies in pan and bake brown.
— Mrs. F. C. Kraemer.

Brown Cookies

One cup white sugar, 1 cup lard or butter, 1 egg, a half teaspoon soda dissolved in a little black coffee, ½ teaspoon cloves, ¼ teaspoon allspice, 1 teaspoon cinnamon, a teaspoon of ginger and a pinch of salt. Mix in flour to handle well, shape in the hand and put a nut in the top of each cake.
— Mrs. F. C. Kramer.

Chinese Cookies

Two cups pastry flour, ¼ cup butter, ¼ cup lard, 2 cups brown sugar, ¼ teaspoon soda, 1 teaspoon vanilla and 2 teaspoons cold water. Mix well and form into little balls about the size of a nutmeg. Place about 4 inches apart in an unbuttered pan and bake about 20 minutes in a moderate oven. When done let stand in a pan about 5 minutes, then remove carefully.
— Mrs. Albrecht.

Filled Cookies

One cup brown sugar 1 cup white sugar, 1½ cups shortening (part lard and part butter) 3 eggs beaten, 1 teaspoon soda dissolved in scant J cup hot water, 2 cups flour, 6 cups oatmeal. Put oatmeal through food chopper.

Filling. — One package raisins, 1 package dates, put through food chopper, add 1 cup sugar, enough hot water to make soft, add 1½ teaspoons vanilla; roll the cookies, cut and place a tea-

spoonful of the filling on cookie then place another cake on top. Press the edges well together and bake.
— Mrs. H. W. Bruedigam.

Filled Fig Cookies

One cup sugar, ½ cup lard, ½ cup milk, 2 cups flour, 1 egg, 2 teaspoons baking powder.

Filling. — Boil until thick 2½ cups chopped figs or raisins, 2 cups sugar, 1½ cups boiling water, 3 tablespoons flour. Roll out dough as thin as possible, then place a layer of dough in a greased pan, spread filling on dough and cover with another layer of dough. When baked cut into squares.
— Mrs. O. Braun.

Honey Drop Cookies

One-half cup butter, ½ cup sugar, 1 cup honey, 2 eggs, 1 lemon (rind and juice), 3 cups flower, 1 teaspoon soda. Drop dough by teaspoons buttered tins and bake in moderate oven.
— Mrs. W. C. Hinrichs.

Cookies

Two cups sugar, ¾ cup butter, 2 eggs, 1½ teaspoons nutmeg, 1 teaspoon lemon extract, ½ cup rich milk, 3 heaping cups flour with 2 teaspoons baking powder, mixed. Mix all well together with spoon, adding a little more flour, if needed, when rolling out. Roll out thin. This makes about 6 to 7 dozen. Bake in hot oven. — Mrs. Klipp.

Plain Cookies

Three eggs, 3 cups flour, 1½ cups sugar, 1 cup butter, 2 teaspoons baking powder, 6 tablespoons milk, nutmeg. Roll thin. Bake quickly.
— Mrs. John C. Koebel.

Sugar Cookies

One and one-half cups sugar mixed with 1 rounding cup (hard) lard, 2 eggs, 1 cup buttermilk, 1 teaspoon soda stirred in the buttermilk, 1 teaspoon baking powder. Flavor with nutmeg. Enough flour to make a soft dough. Bake in a hot oven.
— Mrs. Rausch.

Sugar Cookies

One pound flour, ½ pound butter, ½ pound sugar, 3 eggs. Work flour and butter together thoroughly in mixing bowl, flavor with a little cinnamon or the rind of a lemon, add sugar and eggs ; mix well, and knead into the shape of pretzels.
— Mrs. D. Wagner.

White Cookies

Two cups sugar, 1 cup butter, 1 cup sour cream, 2 eggs, pinch salt, 1 teaspoon baking powder; mix with cream; flavor to taste. Use enough flour to make soft dough, roll, and cut into cookies.
— Mrs. Albrecht.

WINE COOKIES

One-half pound butter, 1 pound sugar, 3 eggs, rind of 1 lemon, 3 teaspoons of rose water, 1 glass wine, 2 teaspoons baking powder and flour enough to roll.
-Mrs. H. W. Bruedigam.

NUT COOKIES

ALMOND COOKIES

One pound shortening (lard or butter), 1½ pounds sugar, 3 eggs beaten, juice of ½ lemon, ½ pound almonds chopped fine, ½ cup milk (large), 2 pounds flour, 2 teaspoons baking powder. Mix to a stiff dough and let stand over night, but do not allow it to get too cold. In the morning roll out thin and bake.
-Mrs. W. C. Westphal.

SMALL ALMOND COOKIES
Two large eggs, ½ pound white flour, ½ pound granulated sugar, ½ pound chopped almonds, 2 ounces butter, grated rind of 1 lemon. Cream the sugar and butter, then add the eggs, a little cinnamon and almonds, stir J hour, then add flour, roll in small balls and bake in slow oven.
— Mrs. Tischer.

Cookies (Kisselsteine)

Two eggs, ½ pound butter, ½ pound sugar, vanilla, ¼ pound almonds, citron, currants, 1 wineglass brandy, flour to roll in little balls; roll in sugar and bake.
— Mrs. H. Tischer.

Butter Cookies

One pound butter, 1½ pound sugar, ½ pint cream, 3 eggs, pinch of salt, ½ pound almonds chopped, ½ teaspoon baking powder, vanilla, flour enough to roll thin.
— Mrs. F. Nyendorf.

Filbert Cookies

Two pounds filberts, grated (weighed with shells), 1 pound powdered sugar, whites of 4 eggs ; stir sugar and eggs for 20 minutes, then add nuts, roll in hand into small balls. Bake in a slow oven; make a frosting of powdered sugar and milk and spread a little on top when baked.
— Mrs. Piepho.

Nut Drops

Four cups sugar, 4 eggs, 4 cup nuts, 2 cups flour, drop them with a spoon and bake in slow oven.
— Miss L. Gansz.

Nut Wafers

Cream well together ¼ cup butter and ¼ cup powdered sugar; add 1 egg well beaten, 1 cup flour and 1 cup finely chopped nuts, walnuts or hickory nuts preferred. Drop small spoonfulls on buttered tins and bake in a moderate oven.
— Mrs. R. Albrecht.

Peanut Cookies

Shell, remove skins and chop 1 quart of peanuts ; there should be one cup. Mix and sift 2 cups flour, ½ teaspoon salt and ½ teaspoon soda, and add 1 cup brown sugar, then add I cup melted shortening, 1 egg well beaten, ½ cup sour milk, 1 teaspoon vanilla and ¾ of the nut meats. Drop from tip of spoon on a well buttered sheet and sprinkle with remaining nut meats. Bake in a moderate oven.
— Mrs. O. A. Skibbe.

Lizzie's Hermits

One cup butter, 3 cups brown sugar, 4 tablespoons sweet milk, 4 eggs, 2 teaspoons soda, 2 cups currants, 1 cup dates cut fine, 1 cup nuts, 1 teaspoon grated nutmeg, 1 teaspoon cinnamon, 1 little grated orange peel, 6 cups flour. This makes a large batch and keeps a long time. Drop in buttered tins some distance apart.
— Mrs. W. C. Hinrichs.

Rock Cookies

One and one-half cups of sugar, 1 cup butter, 3 eggs, 1 pound of walnuts chopped fine, 1 pound dates or raisins, cut fine, 1 teaspoon of soda dissolved in 1 tablespoon of warm water, 1 teaspoon cinnamon, 1 teaspoon cloves, 1 teaspoon allspice, about 2 cups flour. Mix all together and drop on tins.
— Mrs. E. Koretke.

Russian Rock Cookies

One cup butter, 1 cup granulated sugar, ½ cup brown sugar, 1 teaspoon soda dissolved in ½ cup warm water, 3 eggs, broken in, one at a time, 1 teaspoon cinnamon, 1 teaspoon allspice, 3 cups flour, 1 package dates, f pound shelled walnuts, 1 pound peanuts and 1 package raisins chopped. Drop from teaspoon.
— Mrs. F. Nyendorf.

Oatmeal Cookies

Melt ¾ cup butter, work in 1 cup sugar, 2 eggs beaten light, 4 tablespoons milk, 1 level teaspoon baking soda, a pinch of salt, 2 cups flour, 2 cups oatmeal, 1 cup raisins dredged with flour. Drop on greased tins and bake.
— Mrs. William Schilke.

Oatmeal Cookies

One cup brown sugar, 1 cup shortening, 2 eggs, 1 cup milk, 2 cups flour, ½ teaspoon salt, 2 teaspoons baking powder, 1 cup raisins, 2 cups raw rolled oats. Cream sugar and shortening, add eggs (well beaten), and milk. Measure flour after sifting, then sift again with salt and baking powder. Beat into egg and sugar, add raisins (chopped fine), then the rolled oats. Drop by spoonfuls on a cookie sheet. Bake in a hot oven.
— Mrs. Ehlenfeld.

Fruit Cookies
Mix together 1 cup butter, 2 cups sugar, 2 cups currants and chopped raisins, 2 eggs, 2 tablespoons cinnamon, 1 teaspoon nutmeg, 1 scant teaspoon cloves, 1 teaspoon baking soda dissolved in 2 tablespoons sour milk, flour enough to roll out and cut.

Christmas Cookies
One-half pound butter, ½ pound lard, 1 pound brown sugar, 1 cup white sugar, ½ pound citron, chopped real fine, 1 quart molasses, 2 eggs, 1 teaspoon soda, 1/2 pound almonds, chopped fine. Flour enough to roll.
— Mrs. E. J. Keuer.

Christmas Cookies (Lebkuchen)

One cup butter, 1 cup lard, 2 cups hot water, 1 pound brown sugar, 1 quart molasses, ½ pound citron (cut small), ½ pound almonds (chopped fine), 2 teaspoons baking soda, 1 nutmeg, 2 teaspoons cinnamon, 1 teaspoon ginger, 1 teaspoon cloves, ½ teaspoon allspice, 3 cups of flour. Let this stand from three days to a week, then roll and cut in diamond shape with one-half almond in center.
— Mrs. William Schilke.

Pepper Nuts (Pfeffernüsse)

One cup sugar, 2 cups molasses, 1 cup buttermilk, 1 cup shortening, 1 teaspoon soda, 1 teaspoon ginger, ½ teaspoon allspice, ½ scant teaspoon black pepper, 1 teaspoon cinnamon, ½ teaspoon salt, 2 eggs. Enough flour to handle.
— Mrs. Rausch.

Pepper Nuts (Pfeffernüsse)

Two pounds white sugar, 8 eggs, 1 tablespoon ground cinnamon, 1 tablespoon allspice, 1 tablespoon cloves (ground), nutmeg, 1 ounce of citron cut fine, and ½ pound almonds blanched and chopped, a pinch of soda dissolved in a little hot water and flour enough to make a good stiff dough. Roll out and cut with a small round cutter. This dough must be prepared the night before. Bake in a medium oven.
— Mrs. F. C. Kramer.

Pepper Nuts (Pfeffernüsse)

One-half pound butter, ½ pound lard, ¾ pound brown sugar, ¾ pound granulated sugar, 1 pint syrup, ¼ pound almonds, ¼ pound each of candied lemon, orange and citron, 1 egg, ½ lemon, ½ grated nutmeg, 1 teaspoon each of anise seed, mace, allspice, cloves and cinnamon, 10 cents worth of cardamom, 1 teaspoon baking soda dissolved in 2 teaspoons brandy, ½ pint water, flour enough to roll.
— Mrs. Bertha Hass.

Pepper Nuts (Pfeffernüsse) or Christmas Cookies

Four eggs, 2 pounds light brown sugar, 2 cans Karo corn syrup, ½ cup molasses, 1 cup suet, 1 ½ cups lard, 5 cents worth cardamom seed, about the same amount of anise seed, crushed salt to taste. Melt the lard and suet and allow to cool until it begins to harden ; do not heat syrup, mix all cold as possible. Three teaspoons baking powder and 3 teaspoons baking soda dissolved in hot water; add enough flour and knead until it does not stick to the hands. Let stand over night, roll out and cut; bake in a hot oven.
— Mrs. W. Jacobs.

Springerlies

One pound flour, 1 pound powdered sugar, 4 eggs; butter size of an egg, 2 teaspoons baking powder. Roll out thin, cut out and let lay over night. Spread anise seed in pans before putting in cookies and bake very slowly.
— Mrs. H. England.

Cinnamon Stars - Zimtsterne

Whites of 6 eggs, 1 pound pulverized sugar, grated rind of ½ lemon, ⅛ teaspoon ground cinnamon, 1 pound almonds (grated with the peel or put through meat chopper); beat the whites of eggs to a stiff froth, add the sugar and the lemon rind and beat again constantly for 15 minutes. To this mixture add the ground cinnamon and put aside ⅓ of this amount (to be used later for coating). To the quantity remaining add the grated almonds. Roll out and cut with cookie cutter in star shapes. Place in baking tin and spread each star lightly with a little of the mixture that was put aside before. The whole secret of making a success of these delicious cakes lies in the baking. Have the oven quite cool in the beginning. Turn the pan several times and when the cookies appear a pale white then close the oven door and turn on the gas to permit the cookies to bake to a tan shade.
— Marie Doederlein.

SMALL CAKES

Almond Squares

One cup sugar, 3 egg yolks, ¼ cup tepid water, 1 heaping cup flour, 1 scant teaspoon baking powder, lastly the beaten whites of 3 eggs. When cool cut into squares.

Frosting: Cream 1 cup butter, adding gradually as much confectionery sugar as it will take, 1 tablespoon cream, 1 dessert spoon vanilla. Ice squares on all sides and roll in almonds which have been blanched, browned and grated.
— Elizabeth Hass.

Brownies

Two eggs, ½ cup butter, 1 cup sugar, 2 squares bitter chocolate (melted), 1 cup chopped nuts, 1 cup flour, 1 teaspoon vanilla. Mix ingredients together and then spread in buttered pans about ½ inch thick. Bake about 30 minutes; (this will fall). Cut in squares.
— Mrs. E. Perch.

Coconut Cakes

Two teaspoons shredded coconut, 2 eggs, ½ cup butter, ½ cup sugar, 1 cup flour, 1 teaspoon baking powder, and 1 teaspoon vanilla extract. Beat the butter and sugar to a cream; add the eggs, well beaten ; sift in the flour and baking powder and add the coconut and extract. Bake in muffin pans in a moderate oven about 15 minutes. Frost the top.
— Mrs. Albrecht.

Coconut Drops

One cup sugar, ⅓ cup water. Boil to a thread; stir into 2 egg whites. Thicken with coconut. Flavor. Put in oven few minutes to brown.
— Mrs. O. A. Skibbe.

Coconut Macaroons

Two eggs beaten separately, 1 cup sugar, 2 cups oatmeal, 1 cup coconut, teaspoon salt, 1 tablespoon of melted butter, flavor with vanilla or almond. Bake like drop cakes.
— Mrs. J. Semmbow.

Cup Cakes

Eight tablespoons butter or lard, 1 cup sugar, 2 eggs, 1 cup sour milk, 2 cups flour, 2½ teaspoons salt, 1 teaspoon vanilla, 1 teaspoon soda, cream sugar and butter, add beaten egg yolks, then milk and flour. Fold in stiffly beaten egg whites.
— Mrs. F. Nyendorf.

Date Bars

One cup sugar, 3 eggs, 1 cup flour, few grains of salt, 1 heaping teaspoon baking powder, 1 cup walnuts cut, 1 pound dates cut. Beat egg yolks with sugar until creamy; mix flour, baking powder and salt, add nuts and dates. Beat egg whites stiff and stir in. Bake in a shallow pan for 30 minutes. When cool, cut in bars and roll in powdered sugar.
— Mrs. W. J. Keuer.

Date Tarts

One-half pound sugar, ½ pound dates (after stones are removed), ½ pound almonds (not blanched), 3 eggs, bread crumbs. Beat sugar and yolks to a cream, add dates and almonds, which have been mixed thoroughly, then the beaten whites, little vanilla. Roll with hands in bread crumbs, bake in moderate oven, let in pans till cold.
— Mrs. Louise M. Lafrentz.

Kisses

To the whites of 2 eggs add ½ cup granulated sugar and beat 30 minutes, then cut up some dates and stir in, and bake in a very slow oven. Drop on tins, but do not grease the tins. If you should want more, take 4 eggs and 1 cup of sugar and beat 1 hour.
-Mrs. Piepho.

KISSES

One cup corn flakes, 1 cup powdered sugar, 1 cup coconut, 2 eggs (whites). Mix corn flakes, powdered sugar and coconut together with beaten whites of eggs. Bake until light brown.
— Mrs. E. Ferch.

SMALL SPICE CAKES

To 1 cup of molasses add 1 teaspoon soda dissolved in a cup of boiling water, 2 tablespoons melted butter, 1 teaspoon powdered cinnamon, ¼ teaspoon cloves, ¼ teaspoon mace, ¼ teaspoon salt and 3 cups flour. Beat until smooth and bake in gem pans in a moderate oven.
— Mrs. Albrecht.

CREAM PUFFS

One-half cup butter, 1 cup boiling water, 1 cup flour, 4 eggs. Place butter and water in saucepan, on range, as soon as it boils, add flour all at once until well mixed. Stir until it forms a ball and leaves the sides of pan. Set off to cool (not cold) add 1 egg, beat 5 minutes, another egg and beat 5 minutes and so on until eggs are all used up in batter. Drop mixture on oiled shallow pan, bake in moderate oven 40 or 50 minutes. When cool make incision and fill with whipped cream or cream filling. (This should make 15 puffs.)
— Mrs. A. Emde.

CAKE ICINGS AND FILLINGS

BOILED ICING FOR CAKE

Boil together 1 cup granulated sugar and ½ cup water without stirring until it threads quickly when lifted with a spoon; turn this hot mixture slowly into the white of 1 egg that has been beaten to a stiff froth, beat while turning on the hot liquid; continue to beat until stiff enough to spread; add ¼ teaspoon any preferred extract. If the sugar has cooked too much it will grain; then it may be made smooth by beating in a little boiling water; a teaspoonful at a time. — Mrs. A. J. Koehneke.

BUTTER CREAM ICING AND FILLING

One pound powdered sugar, ½ cup butter, 1 teaspoon vanilla, cream. Mix sugar and butter and beat thoroughly, then the cream until it spreads.
— Mrs. Graser.

BUTTER CREAM FILLING AND FROSTING

Beat together 2 heaping tablespoons butter, 6 heaping tablespoons powdered sugar, and 1 tablespoon cream or milk. Beat until light then add ½ teaspoon baking powder and vanilla.
— Mrs. O. Braun.

Chocolate Frosting

One cup confectionery sugar, 2 tablespoons butter, ½ teaspoon vanilla, 2 teaspoons cocoa, 2 tablespoons cold black coffee.
— Mrs. O. T. Lachmann.

Maple Icing

One and one-half cups powdered sugar, ½ teaspoon maple extract, ½ teaspoon butter, 2 tablespoons hot milk.
— Mrs. H. England.

Strawberry Whip

Take 1 pint strawberries, 1 cup sugar, and the white of 1 egg. Beat all together until stiff. Serve on jello or cake.
— Mrs. Chas. Hemler.

Apple Filling

Peel and grate 4 good cooking apples, add ¾ cup sugar, 1 egg yolk, juice of 1 lemon. Beat together and cook about 10 minutes. If not thick enough add 1 scant teaspoon cornstarch dissolved in water.
— Mrs. Klipp.

Boston Filling

Boil 1 cup sugar with 1 cup water until it threads, then beat in the stiffly beaten whites of 2 eggs. Chop 6 figs, 6 maraschino cherries or more, 2 tablespoons walnuts, and stir into the mixture and spread.
— Flora Hemler.

Caramel Filling

Two cups brown sugar, 1 teaspoon flour (rub well in sugar), butter size of walnut, ½ cup cream. Boil altogether until waxy. Flavor with vanilla.
— Mrs. Hunt.

Cocoa Filling

One cup confectionery sugar, 1 teaspoon vanilla, 1 teaspoon cocoa, 1 tablespoon boiled milk. Stir all well together; double the amount if not quite enough.
— Mrs. Klipp.

Coconut Filling

One cup boiling milk, 3 rolled crackers, the yolks of 2 eggs, 4 tablespoons sugar, a pinch of salt; cook a few minutes until thick, remove from fire, add 1 cup coconut and a few drops of almond oil.

Lemon Filling

1 cup sugar, 2 tablespoons flour, 1 egg, 1 lemon (juice and grated rind), 1 piece butter, 1 cup water. Add flour to sugar and mix, then add in egg, lemon, butter and water, and boil until thick.
— Mrs. W. J. Keuer.

Mocha Filling

Two cups powdered sugar, 1 cup sweet butter, 2 tablespoons cocoa, 4 tablespoons hot coffee, 1 teaspoon vanilla.
— Flora Hemler.

Nut Filling

One cup milk, ½ cup granulated sugar, small piece butter, yolk of 1 egg, cup chopped walnuts, cornstarch, vanilla. Let the milk, sugar, butter and egg come to a boil, thicken with cornstarch, add the walnuts, flavor with vanilla. Spread between the layers. If a plain custard filling is desired, omit nuts.
— Mrs. Theo. Doering.

Pineapple Filling

About 1¼ cups to ½ cup pineapples, shredded and the juice, add ½ cup sugar and 1 teaspoon pineapple extract. Boil and thicken with a little cornstarch dissolved in water; boil about 10 minutes.
— Mrs. Klipp.

Tutti Frutti Filling

Make a boiled frosting and when cool add ½ pound almonds and a ½ cup raisins (chopped fine); add a little citron sliced thin. Spread at once.
— Mrs. H. A. Zorn.

German Evangelical Salem Church, Tyrone Township, Le Seuer County, Minnesota, USA.

CAKES

Almond Cake

One cup sugar, scant ½ cup butter creamed together, add yolks of 3 eggs well beaten, 1 cup flour with ¼ teaspoon baking powder and lastly beaten whites of eggs. Spread about 1inch of dough in square tin, then put on a layer of split almonds, brown side up. Sift pulverized sugar over top as soon as taken out of oven.
— Mrs. F. Nyendorf.

Bitter Almond Cake

One pound sugar, 1¼ pounds flour, ¾ pounds butter, whites of 8 eggs, 1 cup milk, 2 teaspoons baking powder, 1 teaspoon almond extract. Bake in loaf tins about an hour, moderate oven.
— Mrs. Schwoerer.

Apple Fruit Cake

Two cups dried apples soaked over night and boil down in 2 cups of molasses. Add 1 cup of shortening, ½ cup of coffee, 2 eggs, 1 cup sugar, ½ cup sour cream, level tablespoon of soda, 2 teaspoons baking powder, 4 cups flour, spices to suit taste, a little salt.
— Mrs. G. Rausch.

Apple Sauce Cake

One and one-half cups brown sugar, ½ cup butter, 2 eggs, 1 cup apple sauce (not sweetened), 1 teaspoon soda, ½ teaspoon cinnamon, ½ teaspoon cloves, 1 cup raisins, 2 cups flour, ½ cup nuts may be added. Bake in loaf tin about 1 hour in slow oven.

Frosting: One cup brown sugar, 3 tablespoons milk, 1 tablespoon butter; cook until it forms a ball in cold water.
— Mrs. Piepho.

Angel Cake

Whites of 8 large or 9 medium eggs, 1¼ cups granulated sugar, 1 cup cake flour, ½ teaspoon cream of tartar, a pinch of salt added to eggs before whipping, flavor to taste. Sift, measure and set aside sugar and flour; whip eggs to foam, add cream of tartar, and whip until very stiff; add sugar and fold in, then flavor and fold in, then flour and fold in lightly through. Put in a moderate oven at once. Will bake in about 25 minutes. It should not take longer, as baking too long dries out moisture and makes them tough and dry. Put in oven too hot for butter cakes and not hot enough for biscuits. If the cake is properly mixed, it will rise above pan. When it is done it begins to shrink ; let it shrink back to level of pan. Watch this stage carefully and when it shrinks back to level of pan, take out of oven and invert immediately, rest on center tube, let hang until perfectly cold, then cut cake loose from around sides and center tube. Knock back slide, insert knife and cut loose from the bottom ; turn out. This must be put in pan that has never been greased.
— Mrs. Albrecht.

Blitzkuchen

One cup sugar, ½ cup butter, 3 eggs beaten separately, ½ cup milk, 2 cups flour, 2 teaspoons baking powder, 1 teaspoon vanilla. Put almonds, sugar and cinnamon on top. Bake in 3 long pans and cut while hot.
— Mrs. F. W. Seeglitz.

Bride's Cake

One scant cup butter, 3 cups sugar, 1 cup milk, 12 egg whites, 1 cup cornstarch, 3 cups sifted flour, 3 tablespoons baking powder, flavoring to taste. Cream butter, add sugar and cream again, alternate with milk and flour; add baking powder mixed with cornstarch, lastly the stiffly beaten whites. Bake in a moderate oven 2 hours, the exact time will depend on the thickness of the loaf.
— Mrs. Albrecht.

Burnt Caramel Cake

Cream ½ cup butter, add 1½ cups granulated sugar gradually, the yolks of 2 eggs well beaten; add slowly 1 cup cold water, then 1½ cups flour; beat well. After this add 3 tablespoons of the burnt sugar, 1 teaspoon vanilla, another cup of flour; beat again, then add 2 teaspoons of baking powder, lastly the well beaten whites of 2 eggs. Bake in 3 layers and put together with boiled icing flavored with 3 tablespoons of the burnt caramel and 1 teaspoon vanilla.
more on next page>

To burn the sugar: ½ cup granulated sugar in skillet, stirred constantly over the fire. It will soften, then melt and finally become liquid, until it throws off an intense smoke. Have ready ½ cup boiling water ; remove sugar from fire, pour water into it, stir quickly, and set back on the fire to boil until about as thick as molasses.
— Mrs. Koehneke.

Cherry Cake

One and one-half cups sugar, ½ cup butter, 1 cup milk, ½ cup nuts, ½ cup maraschino cherries, 1 pinch salt, 1½ cups flour sifted three times, ½ cup flour with two teaspoons baking powder, flavor with vanilla, 4 whites of eggs beaten to a stiff froth, fold in with other ingredients.
— Mrs. E. Ferch.

Citron Cake

Two cups sugar, 6 eggs, ½ pound butter, 2 cups flour, 1 cup ground nuts (walnuts preferred), 1 cup citron and orange peel ground, ½ cup milk, 1 teaspoon baking powder.
— Mrs. H. G. Thoms.

Coconut Sandwich

One cup flour, ¾ cup sugar, 1 teaspoon baking powder, 1 egg, butter size of an egg. Cream butter, add sugar, and egg well beaten, then add flour and baking powder sifted together. Beat well, bake in a layer. When done split open and put lemon cream between. Icing and coconut on top.
— Mrs. O. Braun.

Vanilla Coconut Loaf

One cup sugar, ¾ cup butter, ½ cup milk, beat 3 eggs separately, add another ½ cup milk, 1 teaspoon vanilla, ½ of a small package of coconut, 1 ½ cups flour, 2 teaspoons baking powder, ⅛ teaspoon soda. Medium oven.
— Elsie Rauschert.

Coffee Cake

Two cups light brown sugar, 1 cup butter, 1 cup syrup, 1 cup strong coffee, 4 eggs, 1 teaspoon baking soda, 2 teaspoons cinnamon, 2 teaspoons cloves, 1 teaspoon grated nutmeg, 1 pound raisins, 1 pound currants and 4 cups flour.
— Mrs. Albrecht.

Cornstarch Cake

One cup sugar, ½ cup butter, ½ cup sweet milk, ½ cup cornstarch, 1 cup flour, whites of 6 eggs, a little vanilla, 2 teaspoons baking powder. Cream butter and sugar together, then add milk, then cornstarch and then flour with baking powder. Lastly the 6 beaten whites.
— Mrs. Albrecht.

French Cream Cake

One cup sugar, 3 eggs beaten well, 1½ cups flour, 2 teaspoons baking powder, 3 tablespoons cold water. Bake in two tins. Split cake with knife and fill with following cream: 1 pint milk, 1 egg yolk, 2 tablespoons cornstarch; boil until stiff.
- Mrs. M. Brockman.

Sweet Cream Cake

Ten cent bottle cream, 3 eggs, 1 cup sugar, pinch of salt, 1½ cups flour, 1 heaping teaspoon baking powder, 1 teaspoon vanilla. Mix well and bake in a form tin in a slow oven.

Date Cake

Two eggs, ¾ cup sugar, ½ cup flour, ½ teaspoon baking powder, 1 cup chopped walnuts, 1 cup dates, cut lengthwise. Do not grease pan. Bake 30 minutes slowly. Serve with whipped cream.
— Mrs. J. H. Kalte.

Date Cake

One and one-half cups butter, 1½ cups sugar, 2 large eggs, 1 cup milk, 1 teaspoon baking soda, 1 package dates chopped, 1 cup walnuts chopped fine, 2 cups flour, 1 teaspoon vanilla and a pinch of salt. Mix butter and sugar, add eggs, nuts, dates and vanilla. Add milk in which soda has been dissolved, then flour and salt. Bake in long narrow tins, about 45 minutes in moderate oven.
— Mrs. W. H. Mampe.

French Date Cake

Beat the yolks of 6 eggs with 2 cups sugar, then add the beaten whites of eggs. Beat well ; add 2 cups flour, 2 teaspoons baking powder, ½ pound nuts, 1 pound dates. Cut dates and nuts. Flour both well, then add to batter. Bake 30 minutes in coffee cake tins. This makes two cakes.
— Mrs. W. C. Hinrichs.

Daisy Cake

Beat together 1 cup sugar and 4 egg yolks until very light, stir in ¼ pound butter which has been creamed, and then add 1 gill of water mixed with 3 teaspoons cream, 1 teaspoon vanilla, about 1½ cups flour sifted with 2 teaspoons baking powder. The dough should not be too stiff. Bake in 2 layers. These form the yellow part. For the white part cream together ½ cup butter and 1½ cups sugar, add 1 cup lukewarm water and 2½ cups flour sifted with 2 teaspoons baking powder. Beat hard, then add the juice and rind of 1 lemon and the stiffly beaten whites of 4 eggs. Bake in layers. Put together with a boiled icing filling, alternating yellow and white layers. Use the same icing on top covering it with grated orange peel — when this icing is cold, form a daisy on it of white boiled icing using a pastry tube.
— Mrs. A. Weith.

Economy Cake

One cup water, 1 cup sugar, 1 cup raisins, 1 teaspoon lard, ½ teaspoon cloves, 1 teaspoon cinnamon. Mix and boil 4 minutes, let cool 4 minutes. Add 2 cups flour, 1 teaspoon soda dissolved in ¼ cup warm water, a pinch of salt, nuts if desired. Bake in loaf.
— Elsie Rauschert.

Feather Cake

One and one-quarter cups sugar, ¾ cup butter, ½ cup water, 4 eggs, 2½ cups flour, 2 teaspoons baking powder. Flavor to taste. Cream butter and sugar, add beaten yolks, water, and beaten whites of eggs, then add flour and flavoring and stir hard. Bake in slow oven, either in loaf or layers.
— Mrs. G. C. Hass.

Fruit Cake

One cup seedless raisins, 1 cup dates stoned, each chopped fine, ½ cup butter, 1 cup water. Let boil 5 minutes, cool, and add 1 cup sugar, 1 teaspoon cinnamon, 1 teaspoon cloves, ⅓ teaspoon salt, 1 teaspoon baking powder, 1 teaspoon lemon extract, 2 cups flour. Bake in loaf cake pan in a slow oven for 45 minutes.
— Mrs. Wm. Fredericks.

My Christmas Fruit Cake

One pound brown sugar, 1 pound butter, 8 eggs, 1 pound raisins, 1 pound sultana raisins, 1 pound currants, 1 pound citron, ½ pound figs, 4 apples, 1 tablespoon molasses, 1 cup sour milk, 1 teaspoon soda, 1 teaspoon each of spices, 1 cup good brandy, 1¼ pounds cake flour, 2 teaspoons baking powder. Bake about 2 hours.
— Mrs. O. A. Skibbe.

Fruit Cake

Two and one-half cups sugar, ½ cup butter, 4 eggs, 2½ cups milk, 1 teaspoon vanilla, a little salt, 1 cup citron, 2 cups seedless raisins, 2 cups seeded raisins, 1 cup almonds (chopped fine), 1 teaspoon nutmeg, 1 teaspoon each of ginger and cloves, 1 wineglass each of wine and brandy, 4 teaspoons baking powder, 5½ to 6 cups flour. Bake 1 ½ to 2 hours.
— Mrs. Graser.

Fruit Cake

One pound flour, 1 pound sugar, ¾ pound butter, 2 pounds raisins, 2 pounds currants, 1 pound citron, ½ cup brandy, 8 or 10 eggs, 1 teaspoon mace, 2 teaspoons cinnamon, allspice and nutmeg, 1 teaspoon cloves, 1 tablespoon soda dissolved in ½ cup cold coffee, salt to taste. Stir the butter and sugar to a cream, then the whites and yolks beaten separately, the flour gradually, brandy, spices, lastly the fruit, which should be mixed with part flour.
— Hattie Guelzow.

FRUIT CAKE

One cup sugar, 2 cups flour, ½ teaspoon nutmeg, ½ teaspoon cloves, ½ teaspoon allspice, 1 teaspoon vanilla, 1 tablespoon cinnamon. Mix dry ingredients together, then add 1 wineglass wine, 1½ cups sponge, ½ cup melted butter, ½ cup milk (warm), 1 teaspoon baking soda. Mix and add 1 pound raisins, 1 pound currants, ½ cup chopped nuts, a few chopped cherries (candied), a little citron, lemon peel and orange peel chopped in small pieces. Add 3 eggs, beating the whites to a stiff froth. Let it rise 1 hour and bake 1 hour.
— Mrs. P. Weissbrodt.

WHITE FRUIT CAKE

One cup butter, 2 cups sugar, 1 cup milk, 2½ cups flour, 7 egg whites, 2 teaspoons baking powder, 1 pound raisins, 1 pound figs, ½ pound walnuts, ½ pound citron, 1 pound coconut. Bake 2 hours.
— Mrs. M. Brockman.

GINGER CAKE

One cup dark molasses, ½ cup lard, ½ cup sour milk or buttermilk, 1 egg, salt to taste, 2 level teaspoons soda, 1 teaspoon cinnamon, ½ teaspoon ginger, 2 cups sifted flour. Bake in 2 layers and use white frosting.
— Mrs. Chas. Hemler.

Gold Cake

Yolks of 8 large or 9 small eggs, 1¼ cups granulated sugar, ¾ cup butter, ¾ cup water, 2½ cups cake flour, 2 heaping teaspoons baking powder, flavoring. Sift flour once, then measure, add baking powder and sift three times; cream butter and sugar thoroughly; add flavor, water, then flour, then stir very hard. Put in a slow oven at once.
— Mrs. Albrecht.

Graham Cracker Cake

One cup sugar, ½ cup butter, 2 eggs (well beaten separately), 1 cup milk, 1 cup graham crackers rolled fine, 1 cup flour, 2 teaspoons baking powder and 1 teaspoon vanilla.

Filling: One-third of a cup sugar, 1 cup milk, yolk of 1 egg, 1 teaspoon cornstarch, juice of ½ lemon and 1 cup chopped walnut, added last. Boil in double boiler until thick.

Frosting: White of 1 egg, 1 cup confectioners' sugar, butter size of a walnut. Do not beat white of egg separately, but beat all together until nice and creamy.
— Mrs. Wm. Ehlenfeld.

Graham Cracker Cake

Two tablespoons butter, 1 cup sugar, 4 eggs (or less) separated, ½ cup shredded coconut or nut meats, 1 cup milk, 2 cups rolled graham crackers, 2 teaspoons baking powder, vanilla. Cream butter

and sugar, add yolks of eggs and milk. Mix coconut, baking powder and graham crackers rolled fine, and stir into butter mixture. Lastly, fold in beaten whites of eggs. Bake in 2 layers in a moderate oven. Cover with butter frosting, using lemon flavor, and sprinkle with shredded coconut.
— Clare L. Kemnitz.

Ice Cream Cake

Beat the whites of 10 eggs very stiff, add gradually 1½ cups powdered sugar and 1 cup flour and a heaping teaspoon of cream of tartar mixed thoroughly into the flour before sifting it. Bake in jelly pans or layers. Be careful not to let mixture warm before putting into pans.

Filling: One-half pint sweet cream brought to boiling, 1 teaspoon cornstarch dissolved in a little milk, yolks of 3 eggs beaten and 1 tablespoon powdered sugar. While still warm add ½ pound chopped almonds and fill layers with the warm mixture. Insert halved almonds on top of cake. Does not necessarily have to be frosted. This is a delicious cake.
— M. Doederlein.

Jam Cake

One cup sugar, ¾ cup butter, ¾ cup strawberry jam, ⅓ cup sour milk, 1 teaspoon baking soda, 3 eggs, 2 cups flour, 1 teaspoon cinnamon, 1/4 teaspoon nutmeg. Cream butter and sugar, add beaten yolks, jam, sour milk mixed with the soda flour and spices, then the beaten whites of the eggs.
— Mrs. G. C. Hass.

Delicious Jelly Roll

Take 3 eggs, 1 cup flour, 1 teaspoonful baking powder, 1 cup sugar, 1 teaspoonful vanilla. Bake in good size square pan. When done, place on wet towel, spread with jelly or jam and roll carefully.
— Mrs. Anna A. Jaekel.

Layer Cake

One-half cup butter, 1 cup sugar, 2 eggs, 2 cups flour, 2 teaspoons baking powder, ⅔ cup cold water. Flavor to taste.
— Mrs. J. Rausch.

Sour Milk Layer Cake

Cream 1¾ cups of sugar with ½ cup of butter, add 3 eggs and beat the batter hard. Stir in a cup of sour milk into which a generous pinch of baking soda has been beaten. Last of all, whip in lightly 3 cups of flour that has been sifted with 2 teaspoons of baking powder. Bake in three layers and put together with any kind of icing or filling.
— Mrs. J. Rausch.

Loaf Cake

Three eggs, whites — yolks beaten separately, whites added last, 1 cup sugar, ⅓ cup butter, ⅔ cup milk, 2 cups flour, 1 teaspoon baking powder.
— Mrs. Semmlow.

Fairy Loaf Cake

Four eggs beaten separately, 1¼ cups sugar, ¾ cup butter, ½ cup sweet milk, 2½ cups flour, 1 teaspoon cream tartar, ½ teaspoon baking soda, and flavor to taste. Sift flour once, then measure, add soda, and sift three times. Cream butter and sugar thoroughly, beat yolks to a very stiff froth and stir in, add milk, whip whites to foam, add cream of tartar and whip until very stiff, and add to first mixture. Then add flavoring, then flour and stir very hard. Put in a slow oven at once. Will bake in 30 to 50 minutes.
— Mrs. F. Feig.

Grape-Nuts Loaf Cake

One cup Grape-Nuts, 2½ cups flour, 3 eggs, 1 cup milk, ½ cup butter, 1½ cups sugar, 2 teaspoons baking powder, 1 teaspoon vanilla. Cream butter and sugar, add egg yolks well beaten, then milk and Grape-Nuts; beat well, fold in alternately the stiffly beaten whites of eggs and flour sifted with baking powder. Bake 35 minutes in a moderate oven.
— Mrs. H. A. Zorn.

Imported Loaf Cake

Beat ¾ pound butter and 7 ounces sugar 25 minutes. Add a pinch of salt, 7 tablespoons lukewarm milk, 5 eggs beaten separately, 3 level teaspoons baking powder, 14 ounces flour. Bake 1 hour.
— Mrs. Sodeman.

Marble Cake

Boil until dissolved, 1 tablespoon sugar, 1 tablespoon milk, 1 square chocolate (grated), set to cool. Mix 1 cup sugar, ½ cup butter, 1 egg, 1 cup milk, 2 cups pastry flour (sifted twice), 2 teaspoons baking powder, flavor with vanilla. Add the chocolate to one half of the dough, drop one large spoonful of the chocolate mixture then one of the other mixture and so on. For second layer drop the dark on the light and the light on the dark mixture. Bake in well buttered pan in a moderate oven. This makes a loaf or small layer cake.
— Mrs. Mamie Gruhn.

Inexpensive Marble Cake

Cream ½ cup shortening with 1 cup sugar; add a pinch of salt, the well beaten white of 2 eggs, 1 cup milk, and 2 cups flour sifted twice with 2 tablespoons baking powder. When the dough is well mixed, put half of it in another bowl for the white part of the cake. Then add to what is left, 2 teaspoons each of cinnamon, cloves and allspice, this making the dark part of the batter. Drop the dark and light mixtures alternately by the spoonful into a well greased floured cake tin.
— Mrs. Anna A. Jaekel.

Nut Cake

Two cups sugar, 1 cup milk, ⅔ cup butter, 3 cups sifted flour, 3 eggs, 2 teaspoons baking powder, 1 cup nuts. Cream butter and sugar, add yolks of eggs, milk, then baking powder and flour,

and chopped nuts. Lastly add whites of eggs beaten to a stiff froth. Bake about 45 minutes in a medium oven.
— Mrs. E. Ferch.

HICKORY NUT CAKE

One-half cup butter, 1 cup sugar, whites of 3 eggs, ½ cup milk, 1 ½ cups flour, ¾ cup chopped hickory, walnut or pecan meats, 1 teaspoon cream of tartar, J teaspoon soda dissolved in 1 teaspoon milk. Cream the butter well with sugar, stir in the whites beaten stiff and beat until light and smooth; add milk and flour, alternately and continue stirring; add nuts, stir, then sprinkle the cream of tartar over the mixture and lastly stir in the soda dissolved in 1 teaspoon milk. Beat again and then place in well buttered and slightly floured loaf pan and bake in a moderate oven.
— Mrs. O. A. Kleppish.

MAPLE-NUT CAKE

One-third cup shortening, 1 cup brown sugar, ½ cup milk, 1½ cups flour, 2 teaspoons baking powder, 2 eggs, 1 teaspoon vanilla, 1 cup chopped nuts, J teaspoon salt. Cream shortening and sugar, add yolks of eggs and milk. Beat well, then add flour, salt and baking powder. Fold in beaten whites of eggs last. Bake in loaf about 35 to 45 minutes.
— Mrs. H. England.

WHIPPED CREAM NUT CAKE

Cream 1 cup sugar with 2 tablespoons of lard, or margarine, add yolks of 2 eggs, 1 teaspoon vanilla, ¾ cup sweet milk, 2 cups flour sifted with 2 teaspoons baking powder, a pinch of salt, ¼ cup finely chopped nuts and the beaten whites of 2 eggs.

FILLING: One bottle cream whipped, 1 tablespoon confectioners' sugar, ¼ cup chopped nuts.
— Elsie Rauschert.

ORANGE CAKE

One-half cup butter, 2 cups sugar, 4 egg yolks, the juice and grated peel of 1 large orange and a cup of cold water and 3 cups flour, the whites of the 2 eggs beaten stiff, 2 heaping teaspoons baking powder.

FROSTING: Into the whites of eggs beat 2 cups powdered sugar and when smooth and white flavor with orange juice and a few drops of lemon and grated peel of orange. Spread on cake.
— Mrs. Piepho.

PLAIN CAKE

One-half cup butter, 1 cup sugar, 2 eggs, 1 cup sour milk, 1 teaspoon soda, 1 cup raisins, 2½ cups flour, 1 teaspoon cinnamon, ½ teaspoon cloves. Cream butter and sugar; add well beaten eggs. Dissolve soda in 2 teaspoons cold water, and beat it into the sour milk. Combine the mixtures, add spices and flour gradually. Cut raisins and add. Bake 45 minutes in a slow oven. This mixture makes 1 loaf.

— Mrs. Ehlenfeld.

Plain One Egg Cake

Cream good 1 cup of sugar, 1 tablespoon of butter, then add the yolk of 1 egg. Sift 2 cups of flour and 2 teaspoons of baking powder several times. Take 1 cup of milk and gradually add the milk and flour to the above mixture. Add any flavoring. Fold in the stiffly beaten white of an egg. Have oven real hot when you put the cake in, then turn low. Bake about 20 minutes. This can be baked as loaf, layer or cup cake and varied by adding either currants, raisins, figs, dates, nuts, cocoanut or chocolate.

— Mrs. A. J. Lottes.

Pork Cake

One pound fat salt pork chopped fine dissolved in 1 pint boiling water, 3 cups brown sugar, 1½ cups molasses and syrup mixed, 1 pound raisins (light), 1 pound raisins (dark), 2 tablespoons cinnamon, ½ teaspoon cloves, 1 teaspoon baking soda, 2 teaspoons cream of tartar, 1 nutmeg, 7 cups flour, 5 cents citron, 15 cents shelled walnuts, 10 cents figs, 10 cents dates; citron, nuts, figs, dates chopped fine. Mix all together and bake 2½ hours in moderate oven. This makes three cakes. If desired, ½ cup brandy may be added.

— Mrs. E. Koretke.

PORK CAKE

One pound of fresh salt pork, chopped, ½ pint of boiling water, 1 cup molasses, 2 cups brown sugar, 3 eggs, 1 teaspoon soda mixed with flour, 1 teaspoon cinnamon, 1 teaspoon cloves, 1 teaspoon nutmeg, 1 pound raisins, 1 pound currants, 1 pound nuts, 1 pound dates, citron, 2½ cups flour. Bake in slow oven 1 ½ hours.
— Mrs. R. Baur.

HALF-POUND CAKE

One cup butter, 1 ½ cups powdered sugar, ½ cup milk, 2 cups flour, 2 teaspoons baking powder, 4 eggs. Cream butter and sugar, add well beaten yolks, then milk and flour, and finally the stiffly beaten whites and baking powder. Bake in a moderate oven until light brown. — Mrs. A. Braun.

POUND CAKE

Cream 1 cup of butter and 1 cup of sugar, add 4 eggs beaten separately, then 1 cup milk, 2 cups flour, 2 teaspoons baking powder. The longer the butter and sugar are beaten the better the cake.
— Mrs. M. C. Kretchmer.

POUND CAKE OR ALMOND LOAF

Three-fourths of a pound of butter (scant), ¾ pound sugar, 4 eggs (yolks and whites beaten separately), ½ pound flour, sifted

well with ¼ pound cornstarch, ¼ pound almonds (chopped fine). Flavor to suit. Frost the cake and use some of the almonds whole to ornament the top. Cream, butter and sugar, add yolks that have been beaten well, next flour and cornstarch and almonds, lastly the beaten whites. Beat the cake for about 30 minutes until light. Bake in moderate oven for 1 hour.
— Mrs. A. Streger.

Pound Cake

Wash and drain ½ pound butter. Beat it with the hand until it is quite creamy, then add ½ pound sugar. Beat it until it is like the lightest and whitest hard sauce ; then add 1 egg, beat it until it is quite incorporated, then add another and beat again, and so on until 5 eggs are used. Take great care that each egg is incorporated before the next is added. This requires from three to five minutes beating between each egg, according to how vigorous or slow your strokes are. The success of the cake depends on sufficient beating. When eggs, sugar and butter look like thick, yellow cream, add gradually a small sherry glass of wine or brandy and ½ wine glass of rose water. Mix well together, then sift into the ingredients ½ pound of the finest flour well dried and very slightly warmed, to which ¼ teaspoon salt has been added. Line a round cake pan (with upright sides) with buttered paper neatly fitted, and pour the batter into it and sift powdered sugar over the surface. Bake this cake 1½ hours in a very slow oven. Lay a cardboard over the top for the first hour, which may then be removed and the cake allowed to brown slowly. In turning, be very careful not to shake or jar it.
— Mrs. Albrecht.

Prince Albert Cake

One cup sugar, ½ cup butter, 1 egg, 1 cup milk, 1 teaspoon soda, scant 2 cups flour, 1 teaspoon cinnamon, ½ teaspoon cloves, ½ cup chopped raisins.
— M. Hemler.

Prune Cake

One cup sugar, ½ cup butter, 2 cups flour, 1 cup sour milk, 3 eggs, 1 teaspoon baking powder, 1 teaspoon baking soda, 1 cup prunes (chopped fine), 10 cents worth of walnuts (chopped fine).
— Mrs. William Blanchard.

Southern Cake

Three-quarter cup raisins, ¾ cup dates, ½ cup nuts, 1 teaspoon baking soda dissolved in 1 cup boiling water, pour on fruit and let cool, ½ cup butter, 1¼ cup sugar, 1 teaspoon vanilla, 2 eggs well beaten with butter and sugar, add fruit and 2 cups flour.
— Mrs. L. Langfeld.

Delicate Spice Cake

Two-thirds cup butter, ⅔ cup sugar, 2½ cups flour, 1 egg, 1 cup molasses, 1 cup milk, 2 teaspoons baking powder, 1 tablespoon mixed ground spice, pinch salt, 1 cup raisins. Beat egg, add sugar. Add mixed flour, baking powder and salt, spices, molasses and raisins. Bake in quick oven.
— Mrs. C. H. Massow.

Egg-less Spice Cake

One cup sugar, ½ cup butter, 1 cup sour milk, 2 cups flour, ½ teaspoon salt, 1 teaspoon cinnamon, ½ teaspoon cloves, ¼ teaspoon nutmeg, 1 cup chopped nuts or raisins.
— Mrs. Semmlow.

Sponge Cake

Yolks of 3 eggs well beaten, add 1 cup sugar and beat very hard, add 4 tablespoons cold water, 1 cup flour sifted with 1 teaspoon baking powder, ½ teaspoon vanilla and ½ teaspoon lemon, beat 2 minutes, then add beaten whites of 3 eggs. Bake in slow oven about 30 minutes.
— Mrs. G. C. Hass.

Sponge Cake

Beat yolks of 2 eggs light, beat whites of 2 eggs light. Add ½ cup flour and 1 teaspoon baking powder and a pinch of salt. Do not grease tins. Bake in moderate oven; flavor to suit.
— Mrs. G. H. Rausch.

Hot Water Sponge Cake

Beat yolks of 4 eggs until light and thick, add gradually ½ cup sugar and continue beating. Then add 4 tablespoons hot water, ½ teaspoon almond extract. Beat whites stiff with pinch of salt, add ½ cup sugar, 1 teaspoon cream of tartar and beat again. Add to the first mixture, beating all of the time, then fold in 1 cup flour with 1 teaspoon baking powder. Sift flour and sugar 5 times. Bake in ungreased pan 30 minutes.
— Mrs. F. Nyendorf.

Prize Hot Water Sponge Cake

Yolks of 5 eggs beaten light, 1 cup granulated sugar, 4 tablespoons hot water, 1 cup of flour, 1 teaspoon baking powder, 1 teaspoon vanilla, whites of eggs beaten stiff, sift sugar and flour 5 times. Bake from 45 minutes to 1 hour in a slow oven.
— Mrs. R. Baur.

Loaf Sponge Cake

Four eggs, 2 cups sugar, 1 cup boiling water, 2¾ cups flour, 1½ teaspoons baking powder, ½ teaspoon lemon extract. Beat the yolks of the eggs very light, beat in gradually the sugar. Add the beaten whites of the eggs and boiling water. Beat in very lightly the flour and baking powder well sifted together. Flavor. Bake in a loaf pan in moderate oven.
— Mrs. C. H. Massow.

Cornstarch Sponge Cake

Four eggs, 1½ cups sugar, ¾ cups boiling water, 2 cups flour, 3 teaspoons baking powder, 1 teaspoon cornstarch. Beat eggs and sugar 20 minutes, then add boiling water, flour, baking powder, and cornstarch. Bake in layers or loaf.
— Miss Helen Wollerman.

Potato Flour Sponge Cake

Six eggs beaten separately, 1 cup sugar (½ the sugar beaten with the yolks and ½ with the whites), ¾ cup potato flour, 1 teaspoon baking powder.
— Mrs. M. Brockman.

Olinda's Sunshine Cake

One cup flour, 6 eggs, 1 good cup sugar sifted 3 or 4 times. Beat the yolks of the eggs to a cream. Beat whites very stiff, and add 1 level teaspoon cream of tartar, before quite finished beating. Add the sugar, then the yolks of eggs, 1 teaspoon vanilla, then fold in flour. Bake in very slow oven 30 to 45 minutes.
— Mrs. C. Feig.

Raisin Cake

One cup brown sugar, ½ cup butter, 1 cup raisins (ground), 1 cup boiling water, 1½ cup nuts, 1½ cup flour, 1 egg (not separated), 1 teaspoon baking soda. Mix together and bake in a loaf about 30 to 45 minutes in a medium oven.
— Mrs. E. Ferch,

SCRIPTURE CAKE

Judges 5, 25	1 cup
1 Kings 4, 22	3½ cups
Jeremiah 6, 20	2 cups
1 Samuel 30, 12	2 cups
Matthew 10, 42	1 cup
1 Samuel 25, 18	1 cup
Genesis 43, 11	1 cup
Isaiah 10, 14	6
Leviticus 23, 17	2 teaspoons
2 Chronicles 9,	9
Psalms 19, 10	1 teaspoon
Judges 9, 13	1 glass

Season to taste. Directions in Numbers 11, 18.
— Mrs. H. A. Zorn.

WASHINGTON CAKE

One cup butter, 3 cups brown sugar, 1 cup milk, 4 eggs, 1 cup raisins, 1 teaspoon each of cinnamon, allspice and cloves, 3 cups flour, 2 teaspoons baking powder.
— Miss G. Jacobs.

WATERMELON CAKE

One cup sugar, ½ cup butter, whites of 3 eggs stiffly beaten added last, ½ cup sweet milk, 2 cups flour, 1 teaspoon vanilla, 1 teaspoon baking powder. Pour one-third of this batter into

another dish and add red food color, and a handful of seeded raisins. Bake in a round loaf with the pink in the center. Ice with green frosting.
— Flora Hemler.

CHOCOLATE CAKES

Chocolate Cake

Cream ½ cup butter and 1½ cups sugar, add 4 yolks of eggs beaten. Two squares chocolate dissolved in 5 tablespoons boiling water, ½ cup milk, 1⅔ cups flour, 1 teaspoon baking powder. Lastly add beaten whites of eggs. Bake in three layers. Use butter cream filling.

Chocolate Frosting : Two squares chocolate, 4 tablespoons hot water 2 tablespoons butter, ½ cup sugar, ½ cup milk, which should be added after the above ingredients have been dissolved over hot water. Cook until consistency of thick cream. Remove from stove and beat until thick enough to spread.
— Mrs. M. E. Guelzow.

Chocolate Cake

One-third cup butter, 1 cup sugar, ¼ teaspoon salt, ¼ cup grated chocolate, 3 eggs, ½ cup milk, 3 teaspoons baking powder,

1 teaspoon vanilla, ½ cup nuts, ½ cup raisins, 1½ tablespoons fruit juice, 2½ cups flour. Add whites of eggs last. Bake in loaf about 45 minutes in moderate oven.
— Mrs. W. C. Hinrichs.

BLACK CHOCOLATE CAKE

Put in double boiler 1 egg yolk, ½cup cold water, ½ cup sugar, ⅓ cake chocolate ; when thickened add 2 teaspoons vanilla, and set aside. Beat together 1 cup sugar, ½ cup butter, and 2 eggs, add ¾ cup sour milk, 1 teaspoon soda, 2 cups flour. Stir the two mixtures together and bake in layers or
loaf.
— Miss Helen Wollerman.

EGG-LESS CHOCOLATE CAKE

One and one-third cups brown sugar, 4 tablespoons butter, 1 cup sour milk, 1 teaspoon soda, ½ teaspoon cream of tartar, ½ cup cocoa, 1¾ cups flour, 1 teaspoon vanilla. Cream the butter, add the sugar and mix thoroughly. Mix and sift the dry ingredients. Add the dry ingredients and the liquid alternately to the butter mixture. Flavor with vanilla. Bake in a moderate over about 20 minutes.
— Mrs. A. J. Koehneke.

Devil Cake

One cup brown sugar, 1 bar German sweet chocolate (grated), 1 teaspoon vanilla, ½ cup water; cook this to a syrup. Add 1 cup brown sugar, ½ cup butter, 3 eggs, ½ cup milk, 2 cups flour, 2 teaspoons baking powder. Bake in layers and use cream or butter filling.
— Mrs. Sodeman.

Devil's Food Cake

Half a cup of grated chocolate, ½ cup sweet milk ½ cup brown sugar. Boil together until as thick as cream, then let it cool ; mix a cup of brown sugar with a half a cup of butter. Add 2 beaten eggs, ⅔ of a cup of milk and vanilla flavoring. Mix well, beat in the boiled mixture and add 2 cups of flour sifted well with 2 teaspoons baking powder. Bake in layers. Put together with a boiled icing.
— Mrs. Ehlenfeld.

Fudge Cake

One cup sugar, ⅔ cup butter, 3 eggs, 1 cup milk, 2½ cups flour, 1 heaping teaspoon baking powder, ¼ cup chocolate, ½ cup chopped walnuts; cream the butter and sugar together, add the cup of milk and then stir in the flour, in which the heaping spoon of baking powder has been sifted. Then stir in the chocolate which has been dissolved by placing in a cup and setting in hot water. Add the nuts and lastly the eggs, which should be beaten, whites and yolks separately.
more>

Fudge Frosting: One and one-half tablespoons butter, ½ cup unsweetened powdered cocoa, 1¼ cups confectioners' sugar, a few grains salt, ¼ cup milk, little vanilla. Melt butter, add cocoa, sugar, salt and milk. Heat to boiling point and boil about 8 minutes. Remove from fire and beat until creamy. Add vanilla and pour over cake to depth of ¼ inch.
— Mrs. Albrecht.

Ice Cream Cake

Cream ½ cup butter and 1 cup sugar, then the well beaten yolks of 2 eggs ; 1 cup milk sift 1½ cups flour with 2 teaspoons baking powder and 2 teaspoons cocoa. Add the stiff whites of 2 eggs. Use butter cream filling.
— Clara Steging.

Mahogany Cake

Part 1: One-half cup of sweet milk, ½ cup of bitter chocolate; boil together until thick, then set aside. Part 2: One and one-half cups sugar, ½ cup butter, ½ cup milk 3 eggs, 2 cups flour, 1 teaspoon soda dissolved in a little hot water. Mix Part 2 thoroughly, then stir in Part 1. Turn in tins. Bake slowly. Use butter cream filling.
— Mrs. Piepho.

French Pastry Cake

Two cups sugar, ½ cup butter, 3 yolks of eggs, ½ teaspoon baking soda dissolved in ½ cup sour milk or cream, ½ cup cocoa dissolved in ¾ cup boiling coffee or water, let it cool; 2 cups of flour, 3 beaten whites of eggs, flavor, if desired.

Filling: Three cups powdered sugar, 6 tablespoons cocoa, 6 tablespoons butter, 6 tablespoons coffee or water boiling.
— Miss J. Villna.

Potato Cake

Two cups sugar, ¾ cup butter, ½ cup chocolate melted, ¾ cup milk, 2½ cups flour, 1 cup mashed potatoes, 2 eggs, 2 teaspoons baking powder. Cream butter and sugar, beat in eggs, add chocolate, milk, potatoes, then the flour sifted 3 times, and baking powder. Beat until light.
— Mrs. O. Braun.

Potato Cake

One cup butter, 2 cups sugar, 4 eggs, 1 cup hot mashed potatoes, ½ cup sweet milk, 5 cents walnuts chopped fine, 1 tablespoon vanilla, 1 teaspoon cinnamon, 1 teaspoon nutmeg, ½ teaspoon cloves, 4 tablespoons melted bitter chocolate, 2 cups flour, 2 teaspoons baking powder and a pinch of salt. Bake in layers.
— Mrs. E. Koretke.

Potato Cake

Two cups sugar, 1 cup butter 4 eggs, ½ cup chopped almonds, 2 tablespoons grated chocolate, 1 cup grated raw potato 2¼ cups flour, 1 lemon peel, 2 teaspoons baking powder, ½ teaspoon allspice, ½ teaspoon cinnamon. Bake in a slow oven for about 45 minutes.
— Mrs. W. R. Ahrens.

Spanish Bun Cake

One and one-fourth cups brown sugar, ¼ cup butter, ½ cup sour cream, 1¼ cups flour, ½ cup raisins, 2 eggs, 1 teaspoon soda, 1 teaspoon vanilla, nutmeg to taste. Use butter cream filling.
— Mrs. Willian Schilke.

Tutti Frutti

One cup sugar, ½ cup butter, 1 egg, ½ cup chopped walnuts, ½ cup chopped dates, 2 small squares bitter chocolate (melted), 1½ cups flour, 1 cup sour milk, 1 teaspoon baking soda dissolved in 1 tablespoon vinegar.
— Mrs, E. Moeller.

Pastry Flour

Five pounds flour, 2 pounds cornstarch sifted 5 times.
—Mrs. Semmlow.

Old German Evangelical Church in Locust Point, Baltimore, Maryland.

THE PILGRIM COOKBOOK

TORTEN

Almond Torte

Nine eggs, ¾ pound sugar, 1 teaspoon vanilla, ½ cup flour, 1 small teaspoon baking powder, ¾ pound grated almonds. Beat the yolks of eggs with the sugar until light and creamy, add vanilla, flour, baking powder sifted with flour. Then beat the whites of the eggs until stiff and add grated almonds. Bake from 40 to 50 minutes in a moderate oven.
— Mrs M. C. Kretchmer.

Apple Sauce Torte
A delicious cake that requires no baking.

Stew 6 large apples, as for apple sauce, using very little water, the sauce should be thick, brown 6 cups of crumbs from toast or Zwieback nicely in butter or lard. Press a layer of crumbs in a cake tin, add a layer of apple sauce, then another layer of crumbs; continue until crumbs and sauce are used. Allow cake to stand several hours, then cut and serve with whipped cream.
— Mrs. Eichelkraut.

Blätter Torte

One cup butter, 3 tablespoons sugar, 2 yolks of eggs, 2 cups flour, 1 teaspoon baking powder. Cream butter, sugar, flour and baking powder, then add the yolks of two eggs. Line spring form pan with the above mixture. Take a large can of shredded pineapple, boil and thicken juice with cornstarch and add a little sugar. Put in pan and bake 20 minutes.

Beat whites of five eggs to a stiff froth, and add ½ pound powdered sugar and ¼ pound of chopped almonds; mix and spread on top. Then bake 20 twenty more minutes.
— Mrs. Ferch.

Blitz Torte

One-half cup butter, ½ cup sugar, 1 cup flour, 4 egg yolks, 3 to 5 tablespoons milk, 1 teaspoon baking powder. Spread in two deep layer tins. Beat whites of 4 eggs, add 1 cup powdered or granulated sugar, a little baking powder, and spread this over dough, then sprinkle with ¼ pound chopped almonds. Bake in a medium oven 20 to 25 minutes: test with a straw. Fill with a custard made of 1 egg, 1 cup milk, 1 tablespoon sugar and cornstarch to thicken.
— Mrs. Chas. Storbeck,

Bread Torte

To 9 eggs, beaten well and separately, add 1½ cups sugar; to ½ pound ground sweet almonds add 2 cups bread crumbs, 1 tea-

spoon cinnamon, 1 teaspoon baking powder. Add this to the eggs and sugar. Bake in three layers from 15 to 20 minutes, fill with a cream filling. Let one cup of milk come to a boil then add yolks of 2 eggs, beaten with ¾ cups sugar, add 3 teaspoons cornstarch mixed with a little milk. Cook until it thickens, stirring all the time. When cool add vanilla.
— Mrs. Jacobs.

Rye Bread Torte

Six eggs, 1 cup sugar, 1 cup grated and sifted rye bread, ½ teaspoon cinnamon ½ cup chopped walnuts, a little grated lemon peel, ½ wine glass wine. Beat the yolks and sugar 20 minutes, then add the cinnamon, grated lemon peel, wine, the grated and sifted rye bread and last the egg whites. Bake 45 minutes.
— Helen Wollerman.

Cinnamon Torte

Four tablespoons melted butter, 6 tablespoons sugar, 4 tablespoons milk, 1 cup flour, 4 yolks of eggs, 1 teaspoon baking powder. Bake in spring form.

Custard: Two yolks of eggs, 1 cup milk, 2 tablespoons sugar, 2 teaspoons cornstarch, 1 teaspoon vanilla. Boil until thick and let cool, then put on cake. On top of custard put stiff beaten whites of 6 eggs, to which add 9 tablespoons sugar, ½ teaspoon cinnamon, 1 teaspoon vanilla, ¼ pound chopped almonds. Bake 20 minutes more in slow oven.
— Mrs. H. G. Tischer.

Cherry Torte

Make a dough of ¼ pound lard, ¼ pound butter, 4 tablespoons sugar, 2 teaspoons cinnamon, 2 egg yolks, ½ pound flour, ½ teaspoon baking powder. Work like a pie crust and place in a form with straight sides, bringing dough well up on sides of form. Fill with following custard: 4 eggs, ¾ cup sugar, ¾ cup milk, 1 quart cherries drained of juice. Bake about 1 hour and serve with whipped cream.
— Mrs. A. Piepho.

Date Torte

Two eggs beaten light, add 1 cup sugar, beat well, 1 cup walnuts, 1 cup dates chopped, 3 tablespoons flour, 1 teaspoon baking powder. Bake in square tin Cover with white icing.
— Mrs. F. Nyendorf.

Farina Torte

Five or 6 yolks of eggs, 1 good cup sugar, ¾ cup toast rolled fine, whites of eggs (stiff), ¼ cup of Farina with 2 teaspoons baking powder, J pound chopped walnuts. Bake in 2 layers in hot oven for 10 minutes. Whipped cream frosting and filling.
— Mrs. Albrecht.

French Torte

Mix ½ cup butter, 3 heaping tablespoons sugar, 2 cups flour, 1 whole egg and 2 egg yolks and 1 teaspoon baking powder into a dough and spread in a spring form. Spread strawberry jam on top of dough and put the following on top: ½ pound almonds peeled and chopped, ½ pound powdered sugar, 6 egg whites well beaten, and 1 grated lemon rind. Bake slowly 1 hour.
— Mrs. H. G. Tischer.

Graham Torte

Cream 1 tablespoon butter with 1¼ cups sugar, 2 eggs well beaten, 1 cup sour milk in which has been dissolved 1 teaspoon soda, 34 graham crackers, which have been rolled or ground to crumbs, 1 teaspoon vanilla.
— Mrs. Edward J. Keuer.

Hazelnut Torte

Eight eggs, 2 cups hazelnuts, ground fine (measure before grinding), 1 pint powdered sugar, 1 teaspoon baking powder, grated rind of 1 lemon. Beat yolks of eggs until thick, add sugar after grating rind of lemon on same, then add nuts with baking powder mixed through them, and last whites of eggs beaten stiff. Bake 40 minutes in moderate oven. Served with whipped cream or fruit it is very good.
— Hrs. H. W. Bruedigam.

Himmel's Torte

One-half pound butter, ¼ pound sugar, 3 egg yolks, ½ pound flour, 1 teaspoon baking powder. Bake in three layers. When cold spread layers with currant jelly, then with the following cream: ½ pint sour cream, 2 tablespoons sugar, juice of 1 lemon, vanilla, 2 tablespoons flour, 2 egg yolks. Boil until this is thick. Ice cake with 3 beaten egg whites, powdered sugar, ¼ pound chopped almonds and a little cinnamon. Beat well and spread on top.
— Mrs. H. G. Tischer.

Hot Lemonade Torte

Yolks of 6 eggs, 1½ cups sugar, 1 grated lemon rind, 1½ cups bread crumbs or 2 cups cracker meal, ¼ teaspoon baking powder, ¼ teaspoon cinnamon, ¼ pound almonds (chopped), and the well beaten whites of 6 eggs folded in last. Bake 1 hour and when done pour ½ cup hot lemonade over cake with a teaspoon.
— Mrs. E. A. Bierdemann.

Krumble Torte

Six eggs beaten separately, 2 cups sugar, ½ pound chopped walnuts, ½ pound dates cut, 1 cup bread crumbs, 1 teaspoon baking powder. Bake in 2 tins. After baked, break in small pieces and pour over it whipped cream, which has been sweetened. Bake from 35 to 45 minutes.
-Mrs. E. J. Keuer.

Poppy Seed Torte

Eight eggs (whites added last), ¾ pound powdered sugar, ¼ pound raisins (seedless), ¼ pound currants, ¼ pound walnuts (chopped), ¼ pound poppy seed, 1 teaspoon cinnamon, ½ teaspoon cloves, a little baking powder, grated rind of 1 lemon. Put raisins and currants through chopper, bake 1 hour or more if necessary. Must stand 1 day before cutting. Very good.
— Clara A. Spangenberg.

Potato Torte

Six eggs, ½ cup potatoes, grated, ¾ cup rye bread, grated, 1 cup sugar, ¼ wine glass wine or brandy, a little citron, allspice and almonds chopped, a little baking powder. Bake ¾ hour.
— Clara A. Spangenberg.

Prune Torte

Line the sides and bottom of a deep baking dish with pastry and fill the bottom with soaked, pitted and stewed prunes; sprinkle over them sugar to sweeten, mixed with a tablespoon flour and bake. When thickened slightly, pour over the prunes the yolks of 3 eggs beaten with ½ cup milk and ½ cup each of cake crumbs and sugar. Bake until custard is set; spread with whites of eggs beaten stiff with 3 tablespoons sugar, flavor, and brown.
— Mrs. H. Berger.

Sand Torte

Stir ½ pound butter until smooth, then add the yolks of 6 eggs; then add ½ pound sugar, ½ pound cornstarch and rind of lemon. Stir 15 to 20 minutes. Mix a little cornstarch with 1 teaspoon baking powder, beat the whites and add.
— Mrs. Jacobs.

Sand Torte

One pound unsalted butter, 1 pound powdered sugar, 9 large eggs, 2 cups sour cream, 1 lemon, rind and juice, 1 pound rice flour, 2 cups flour, 2 small teaspoons baking powder. Cream butter and sugar, add eggs then alternately the rice flour, cream, juice and rind of 1 lemon and finally the flour with baking powder. Stir 30 minutes, place into a spring form, bake in moderate oven.
— Johanna Kretchmer.

Schaum Torte

Whites of 6 or 7 eggs, 2 cups sugar (granulated, sifted), 1 tablespoon vinegar, 1 tablespoon vanilla. Beat whites of eggs to a stiff froth, add sugar, vinegar and vanilla. Beat this 30 minutes . Bake in a spring form 1¼ hours, slow oven. When done turn off gas and leave cake in the oven 15 minutes longer. Bake day before using; leave in tin. When ready to serve take out of tin and put fresh or canned fruit on top and whipped cream over fruit. Grease pan with butter.
— Mrs. M. C. Kretchmer.

ICE CREAM AND BEVERAGES

Ice Cream

One quart milk, 1 quart cream, 4 eggs, whites beaten stiff, 2 cups sugar and vanilla to taste. Pack and freeze.
— Olga T. Bohnsack.

Vanilla Ice Cream

One quart whipping cream, 1 cup sugar, 2 eggs well beaten, flavor with vanilla. Freeze.
— Mrs. F. Nyendorf.

Angel Parfait

One pint cream, ½ cup water, ½ cup sugar, 3 egg whites, 1 cup English walnuts or 1 cup candied cherries. Boil sugar and water until it threads, then remove from fire and stir it into the beaten egg whites ; beat well and flavor. When cold gently stir in the cream which has been beaten stiff, add chopped nuts or cherries. Pack in ice and salt 4 hours; do not turn the freezer. One-half cherries and one-half walnuts makes a delicious substitute for 1 whole cup of either. Fine.
— Mrs. William Bohnsack.

Lemon Ice

Four cups hot water, ¼ cup cold water, 2 cups sugar, ½ cup lemon juice, ½ tablespoon gelatine, 1 tablespoon lemon rind. Dissolve gelatine in cold water for 10 minutes. Boil sugar and hot water; after it begins to boil add the gelatine and lemon rind. Pour into mixing bowl and set in pan of ice water; when cold add the lemon juice, strain and freeze.
— Elsa Rauschert.

Lemon Sherbert

One quart milk, 1 pint sugar, juice of 4 large lemons. Flavor with lemon extract, pineapple or any other fruit may be used. Freeze.
— Mrs. F. Nyendorf.

Pineapple Ice

One can crushed pineapple, 2 cups sugar, juice of 4 lemons, 1 pint of water, whites of 1, 2 or 4 eggs, mix and freeze.
— Mrs. R. Baur.

Pineapple Milk Sherbert

Four cups milk, 1½ cups sugar, 2 cups grated pineapple, ½ cup lemon juice. Mix the pineapple, lemon juice and sugar. Add the milk. Then freeze.
— Mrs. F. Nyendorf.

Strawberry Ice

One quart mashed strawberries, 1½ pints of water, enough sugar to sweeten, about 1 cup, juice of 2 lemons. Freeze.
— Mrs. R. Baur.

Grape Nectar

Two cups grape juice, juice of 1 orange, 2 lemons, ½ cup sugar, 1 pint water. Mix and serve ice cold, garnishing with sliced lemon. — Mrs. Chas. Hemler.

Punch

Two cups sugar, 2 cups water, lemon and orange rind. Cook together for 5 minutes and strain. One box strawberries, wash, mash and strain through coarse sieve. Add ½ cup sugar, 1 pineapple grated, 6 lemons, 1 or 2 oranges, ½ cup strong tea, 4 cups water, cracked ice for serving. This serve 25 people or 25 sherbert cups.
— Lydia H. Bohnsack.

Gluehwein

One pint good red wine, 1 cup sugar, 1 cinnamon stick, 6 cloves and the thinly peeled rind of 1 lemon. Let this come to a boil. Serve while hot. — Marie Doederlein.

Flaxseed Lemonade

Into 1 quart boiling water, stir ½ cup whole flaxseed, add the juice of 2 lemons and sweeten to taste. Let this come to a boil. Put in tightly-covered receptacle jar for two hours, when it is ready to drink either hot or cold. This is excellent for colds.

Good Cough Syrup

Five cent cherry wood bark ground and soaked in 1 pint of water over night. In the morning strain and add 5 cents rock candy 5 cent stick licorice chopped fine, and boil until thick like syrup. Dose — 1 teaspoon every hour.
— Mrs. H. England.

JAMS

Apricot Jam

One basket apricots, 5 cups sugar, ½ pint pineapple or 1 cup. Wash and cut apricots and pour on sugar and let stand over night. Then add cut pineapple and cook until thick.
— Mrs. F. Nyendorf.

Blackberry Jam

Boil 4 cups of rhubarb until tender; add 8 pints of blackberries, boil 10 minutes longer, add 6 pints of sugar. Boil 20 minutes and when cool seal in glass jars.
— Mrs. Kramer.

Carrot Jam

Three pounds carrots, 3 oranges, 1 lemon, 5 peaches and a little ginger root. Run carrots and peaches through a shredder. Grate the rind of a lemon and of one of the oranges. Add juice of lemon with the oranges and peaches. Weigh and add as much sugar as you have fruit. Boil over a slow fire for 1 hour.
— Mrs. A. Steging.

Carrot Marmalade

Four cupfuls of grated raw carrots, 2 cupfuls of sugar, 4 tablespoonfuls of lemon juice and a scant teaspoonful of salt. Wash and scrape the carrots, grate or put through a food chopper. Put in a preserving kettle with 2 cupfuls of water and boil slowly for J hour, by which length of time the water will have boiled away. Add the sugar and boil or simmer slowly for 1 hour; add lemon juice and salt. Stir often. Pour into sterilized glasses and cover with paraffin.
— Mrs. A. Steging.

Heavenly Jam

One basket of blue grapes, 3 oranges, 1 lemon, 3 pounds sugar, 1 pound seeded raisins; slip the skins off the grapes, put the pulp in kettle, keep from burning, a few minutes simmering will make the seed come out, put through colander to remove seeds, then add skins. Squeeze juice from oranges and put through meat grinder with peel, add raisins and sugar. Mix all together and cook 20 minutes.
— Mrs. A. Piepho.

Orange Marmalade

Select 1 orange and 1 lemon with a thin skin. Cut in slices and then in cubes. To this add 6 cups of water. Let stand over night. Next morning boil 20 minutes; measure liquid and to 1 cup of mixture add 1 cup of sugar. Boil evenly for 30 minutes, or until it jells. This will make 8 medium sized glasses.
— Mrs. Albrecht.

Pear Conserve

Five pounds pears, 1 quart cranberries, rind of 1 orange, parboiled twice, juice of 2 oranges. Put all through food grinder add 4 pounds of sugar and let stand over night. Next morning boil 45 minutes to 1 hour, and put in tumblers or jars. When cold cover with paraffin and put away to keep.
— Clare L. Kemnitz.

Pineapple and Strawberry Jam

One pineapple cut up fine, 3 boxes of strawberries ; boil together 15 minutes, add 3 pounds sugar and boil 20 minutes longer. Put in glasses and when cold seal.
— Mrs. F. C. Kramer.

Plum Conserve

One basket California blue plums, seeded and put through the meat mill, 4 pounds sugar, 1 pound nut meats (pecans), juice of 3 lemons and 4 oranges and the rind; 2 oranges put through the meat mill. Boil 40 minutes, stirring to keep from burning.
— Mrs. C. B. Moellering.

Raspberry Jam

Four boxes red raspberries 2 quarts rhubarb, cut fine. Cook rhubarb to a pulp without water. Mash berries and add to the rhubarb then cook ½ hour. Now add 2½ quarts sugar and cook 5 minutes.
— Mrs. Ed. Pierce.

Rhubarb Conserve

Five pounds rhubarb, 5 cups sugar, 1 pound figs, 1 pound raisins, 1 pound nuts, juice of 2 lemons. Boil 15 minutes.
— Mrs. R. J. Frank.

Rhubarb Marmalade

Three pounds of rhubarb, 3 oranges, 3 pounds of sugar; cut rhubarb fine, add 1 of sugar, let stand over night; in the morning cook 20 minutes, then add the chopped oranges and the peel of 1 orange. Mix all together and cook 30 minutes.
— Mrs. A. Piepho.

Strawberry Jam

Take 2 quarts berries at a time, pick and wash; use an equal amount of sugar and berries (judging by looks). Boil 20 minutes.
— Mrs. John C. Koebel.

Strawberry Preserve

Four cups of strawberries, 3 cups of sugar, 1 cup of water. Cook berries and water 19 minutes, add sugar and boil 3 minutes or a little longer. Seal in sterilized jars. Use pint jars, and be careful to have good rubbers.
— Mrs. C. Feig.

Elderberry and Grape Jelly

Use ⅓ of ripe grapes and ⅔ of ripe elderberries, have all the stems out, put them in a sauce pan, and place over the fire and let them cook slowly until tender enough to yield all their juice freely, then put it into a jelly bag and let drain until all the juice is out. Then for each pint of juice add 1 pint of granulated sugar. Boil the sugar and juice together and stir until the sugar is dissolved. Continue the boiling until a little of the jelly (cooled) stiffens on a saucer and when it is partly cool pour it into the jelly molds and when cold cover with brandied paper to keep out the air.
— Mrs. Albrecht.

Grape Juice

One basket grapes; cook until cooked apart, strain through bag then add 1 cup sugar, put back on stove to come to a boil, then bottle, and keep in a cool, dark place. When serving put about ¼ grape juice in a glass, then fill with water.
— Mrs. A. Piepho.

Paradise Jelly

Two quarts cranberries, 15 quinces, 15 apples. Cut the apples and quinces without paring, add cranberries, and cover with water. Cook until soft, then drain through a jelly bag. Let juice boil 15 minutes, add sugar and boil 5 minutes longer. Allow 1 cup sugar to 1 cup juice.
— Mrs. F. W. Seeglitz.

THE PROPER TIME TO CAN FRUITS AND VEGETABLES AS THEY COME IN THEIR SEASON.

Apricots and Plums — August 10th to September 10th.
Apples (Pippin are the best) — October 20th to November 20th.
Asparagus — May 15th to July 1st.
Beans — September 20th to October 20th.
Lima Beans — August 20th to October 15th.
Blueberries — July 1st to August 5th.
Blackberries — July 15th to August 25th.
Cauliflower — September 15th to October 25th.
Cherries — June 15th to July 1st.
Currants — June 10th to July 1st,
Corn — August 15th to October 15th.
Pineapples (Sugar loaf are the best; over ripe will not do) —May 10th to July 1st.
Peaches (the late Crawford are the best) — August 20th to October 5th.
Pears — August 20th to October 15th.
Peas— May 25th to July 1st.
Raspberries — July 1st to July 25th.
Rhubarb— May 15th to July 1st.
Strawberries — June 1 to June 25.
Tomatoes — August 15th October 1st.

Fruits and vegetables must never be canned when speckled or frost bitten and should always be kept in the dark and at a temperature of from 45 to 65 degrees. Tomatoes, strawberries and vegetables should be wrapped in brown paper.

CANNED FRUITS AND VEGETABLES

Canned Corn

Cut the corn off the cob and put only enough water with it to make it juicy. Cook ½ hour, then put in 2 tablespoons salt to each quart of corn, boil ½ hour longer and seal tight. When ready to use, freshen in a little water and let simmer about 20 minutes. Pour off the water and put on milk.
— Mrs. G. H. Rausch.

Canned Corn

Six cups of corn cut from the cob, 1 cup water, 1 tablespoon salt, 1 cup sugar. Boil 20 minutes and put in jars; seal while hot.
— Mrs. F. C. Kramer.

Canned Rhubarb

Wash and peel rhubarb; cut in about inch lengths. Put in double boiler with very little water. Let cook thoroughly and can while hot. Do not add sugar until ready to use.
— Mrs. Theo. Doering.

Spiced Rhubarb

To 2½ pounds rhubarb, washed and cut into inch pieces, add 1 cup vinegar, 2 pounds sugar, and 1 tablespoon each of cinnamon and cloves. Put all into a preserving kettle and boil steadily for 30 minutes. Put in jelly glasses, covering the tops with paraffin.

Canned Tomato Soup

One peck ripe tomatoes, 2 medium onions, 3 large stalks of celery; cook until very soft and strain through a fine sieve. Put back to boil, add ½ cup butter, ½ cup sugar, ½ cup flour, 2 tablespoons salt, and a pinch of red pepper. Mix and cook until thick. Seal hot and put in jars. When ready to use, put on to boil, add a pinch of baking soda and 1 quart of milk, serve.
— Mrs. Marie Saul.

Pickled Cherries

Pit the cherries and cover with cold white vinegar; let stand 48 hours. Then drain and put in layers into jars or large bowl, alternating each layer with a covering of sugar. Allow 1 cup sugar to 1 cup cherries. Let stand 1 week and stir twice daily with a wooden spoon. Then put in jars and seal.
— Mrs. C. B. Moellering.

PICKLED PEACHES

Two quarts vinegar 2 pounds sugar, 1 tablespoon whole cloves, tied in a bag, when boiling add peaches ; put 1 clove in each peach. Do not boil peaches too soft; seal air tight.
— Mrs. J. Semmlow.

SAUERKRAUT OR SOUR KRAUT

Twenty large heads of cabbage make 5 gallons, cut out core and cut fine, mix with 1 cup of salt, put several handfuls in jar and press good; keep adding and pressing, cover with a cloth and press down so the scum will be over the cloth. It can be easily removed, put in a plate and heavy weight. When you take out sauerkraut rinse cloth and add a little water if necessary.
— Mrs. J. Semmlow.

KETCHUP, PICKLES, ETC.

Tomato Ketchup

To 1 peck tomatoes add 2 large onions and 1 handful salt. Let boil until soft, then strain through fine sieve. Put on to boil with 2 tablespoons white pepper and 1 grated nutmeg and 1 pint vinegar. Let boil until thick about 3 hours.
— Mrs A. Piepho.

Tomato Ketchup

Boil 1 peck of sliced, unpeeled tomatoes with 6 white onions and cook until so soft that they can be rubbed through a colander; strain through a sieve and return to the fire with 3 bay leaves, a tablespoon each of powdered mace, white pepper, cloves, sugar, salt and ½ tablespoon celery seed tied in a small cheesecloth bag. Boil for nearly 6 hours and stir frequently. Remove the bag of celery seed and pour in a pint of vinegar. Bring again to a boil and remove from fire ; when cold, bottle and seal.
— Mrs. Albrecht.

My Own Tomato Ketchup

One peck of good ripe tomatoes cut or, mash, ½ pound mixed spices, tied in a thin cloth, boil about 1 hour, then strain and boil 2 hours with same spices. Add 1 tablespoon salt, 4 tablespoons ground mustard, ¼ teaspoon red pepper, 1 teaspoon paprika, ½ teaspoon ground cloves, 1½ cups sugar, 2 cups of vinegar. Keep on stove until the last bottle is filled, be sure and have bottle air tight. — Mrs. J. Semmlow.

Chili Sauce

Six onions, 24 ripe tomatoes, 4 green peppers, 3 small tablespoons salt, 9 small tablespoons sugar. Boil gently 3 hours.
— Mrs. R. J. Frank.

Chili Sauce

One peck tomatoes (red ripe), 2 cups onions, 4 green peppers and 1 small red pepper (seeds removed). Grind the above in coarse food chopper. One quart vinegar, ½ cup salt, 4 cups granulated sugar, ½ teaspoon red pepper (ground); put in the above. Put the following spices in a bag: Three teaspoons ground cloves, 3 teaspoons ground cinnamon, 1 small ground nutmeg, ½ teaspoon ground allspice, 3 teaspoons celery seed. Boil 3 hours. Put in glasses or bottles and seal at once.
— Mrs. H. G. Thoms.

Chili Sauce with Celery

Put through food chopper, 15 large ripe tomatoes, 4 large stalks celery, 5 large onions, 1 red pepper, add 8 tablespoons brown sugar, 2 tablespoons salt, 3 cups vinegar. Boil about 2 hours.
— Mrs. F. Nyendorf.

Chili Sauce

Skin 2 dozen large ripe tomatoes, add 2 green and 1 small red pepper, 2 large onions; chip fine and boil until thick. Add 2 cups vinegar, 1 tablespoon salt, 2 cups sugar, 1 teaspoon ginger, 1 teaspoon cloves, 1 teaspoon allspice. Boil 15 minutes or longer. Bottle and seal. Very good.
— Mrs. Marie Saul.

Ripe Cucumbers

Leave cucumbers in salt 4 hours, after peeling and cutting, scoop center with silver spoon, drain in colander. Boil up in ½ vinegar and ½ water, drain in colander again. Take 2 quarts water, 2 quarts vinegar, 2 quarts sugar, mustard seed. Boil all well. Add cucumbers; boil them up. Can while hot. In one or two days pour off juice and boil up again, pour over cucumbers again. This is for 18 cucumbers.
— Mrs. Louise M. Lafrentz.

Senf Gherkins (Mustard Pickles) 2

Peel 1 dozen ripe cucumbers, slice and quarter, removing all seeds and pulp. Cover with well salted water and let stand over night. Rinse well, drain until dry. To 1 quart of vinegar add 2 cups of sugar, 1 tablespoon whole mixed spices in a cheesecloth bag. When boiling add cucumbers, a few at a time. Let come to a boil, then remove to jars; sprinkle with mustard seed, cover with liquid and seal.
-Mrs. Wm. Ehlenfeld.

Cucumber Chowchow

One peck large green cucumbers, 4 large onions: chop fine; salt and let drain over night. Squeeze dry, then add 1 pound brown sugar, 1 quart cider vinegar, 2 tablespoons celery seed, 2 tablespoons white mustard seed, a pinch of red pepper. Let come to boil and seal hot.
— Mrs. Wm. Blanchard.

Corn Relish

One dozen large ears of corn, 12 large white onions, 6 red peppers, medium size head of cabbage, 2 stalks celery, 2 cups sugar, ½ cup salt, 3 quarts vinegar, ½ pound mustard. Boil 30 minutes. Can while hot. — Ella Baerwald.

CORN RELISH

One dozen ears of corn, cut from cob, 8 sweet green peppers, 2 red peppers, 1 quart onions, 1 quart yellow cucumbers, 2 quarts ripe tomatoes, put this through food chopper, except corn. ½ cup salt, 1 quart sugar, 1 quart cider vinegar, 1 ounce celery seed, 1 ounce mustard seed, 2 tablespoons tumeric. Boil 40 minutes and seal in airtight jars. Note: 3 yellow cucumbers equal 1 quart.
— Mrs. F. C. Kraemer.

CORN RELISH

Twelve large ears of corn, 1 large head of cabbage, 8 large onions, 3 small red peppers, 10 sweet green peppers. Remove seeds. Cut corn from cob, cabbage, onions and peppers fine. Add 3 pints of vinegar, 1¼ cups sugar, ½ cup salt. Boil about 15 minutes, then add corn, mix 3 teaspoons mustard with 1 tablespoon flour, dissolve in vinegar. Boil about 15 minutes more. Seal while hot. You may also add ¼ teaspoon tumeric if you have any.
— Mrs. Semmlow.

DILL PICKLES

Wash and scrub medium sized green pickles, and lay them in fresh water over night. In the morning wipe dry, place in half gallon jars, alternately with layers of fresh dill, which has been cut in 2 inch pieces. Into each half gallon jar place 2 small red peppers, or ½-inch ring of large red pepper, 1 large teaspoon of whole black pepper, 2 medium bay leaves, 2 slices of horseradish size of

a quarter. For 18 quarts of pickles, cook 6 quarts water, 1 pound salt, 1 level teaspoonful powdered alum. Let come to a boil, add 4 cups or 1 quart cider or white vinegar. Fill jars of pickles with this boiling fluid put fresh rubber on jar and seal tight. Note: the pickles will go through a fermenting process and if you see bubbles in cans, rest assured pickles are not spoiled.
— Mrs. Arthur Emde.

Mustard Pickles

Two quarts small pickles, 2 quarts small onions, 1 large head cauliflower; soak in salt water over night. Put 3 quarts white vinegar on to boil, to this add spice bag, 1 teaspoon paprika, ¾ pound dry mustard, wet with a little vinegar, ½ cup flour, 1 ounce celery seed, i ounce mustard seed ; then add onion, pickles and cauliflower. Boil until it thickens and when nearly done add 1 pound brow sugar, 3 green peppers, 3 red peppers, cut up small. Very good.
— Mrs. W. A. Sass.

Mustard Pickles

One quart small cucumbers, 1 quart small white onions, 1 quart sliced green tomatoes, 1 quart cauliflower cut in pieces, 4 green peppers cut up, 1 pint celery cut in pieces, 1 pint green or wax beans cut fine. Make a brine of 4 quarts water and 1 pint salt, pour over vegetables and let stand 24 hours. Before you add the celery and beans heat them enough to scald and then drain. Mix 1 cup flour, 4 tablespoons ground mustard, 1 tablespoon turmer-

ic mixed with enough vinegar to make smooth, 1 cup sugar. Add enough cold vinegar to make 2 quarts in all. Boil until it thickens, stirring all the time, add vegetables and let come to a good boil. Seal in glass jars.
— Mrs. Chas. Hemler.

Sweet Mustard Pickles

Select small pickles, soak in salt water over night. Dry each pickle and pack in jars. Make a paste of 2 teaspoons mustard, 1 teaspoon salt, 1½ teaspoons sugar, and cider vinegar to each quart of pickles. Add this paste to enough cider vinegar to cover the amount of jars of pickles. Seal and put away.
— Clare L. Kemnitz.

Olive Oil Pickles

Three dozen small pickles, 8 onions, ¼ cup white mustard, ¼ cup black mustard seed, 1 tablespoon celery seed, ¼ teaspoon red pepper, ½ cup olive oil, 1 large cup sugar. Cover with white vinegar. Slice onions and pickles fine, sprinkle with salt and let stand over night, then drain and mix with other ingredients. Let stand two days, stir often and seal without heating.
— Mrs. F. C. Kramer.

Saratoga Pickles

Ten onions, 25 pickles; slice and sprinkle salt on same and let stand 3 hours or over night, then drain. Bring to a boil 1 quart vinegar, 1 pound sugar, 1 tablespoon celery seed, 1 tablespoon

ground mustard, 1 tablespoon ginger, 1 teaspoon turmeric. Add pickles and boil for 5 minutes. Put in jars and seal.
— Olga T. Bohnsack.

Sliced Pickles

One peck small cucumbers, 30 small onions, 4 green peppers, 2 red peppers. Slice and soak cucumbers over night in strong salt water, rinse good and drain in morning, chop peppers. One and one-quarter gallons vinegar, 6 cups sugar, 5 cents turmeric, 1 tablespoon celery, small lump: alum, 10 cents yellow mustard seed. Boil hard for 5 minutes then add sliced cucumbers and sliced onion and let come to a boil.
— Mrs. Frank.

Picalilli
One-half peck green tomatoes, ¼ peck onions, 6 stalks celery, 1 large cabbage (all chopped fine); 4 tablespoons salt. Let stand 24 hours, then drain. Add vinegar, sugar, mixed spices. Boil, but not long.
— Mrs. Louise M. Lafrentz.

Picalilli
One peck green tomatoes, 6 large onions, 1 large head celery, 3 cups sugar, 1 teaspoon each cinnamon, allspice, mustard, pepper (all ground); 3 pints vinegar, 2 tablespoons salt. Chop or grind and boil 2 hours.
— Mrs. O'Rourke.

Pepper Relish

Two dozen green peppers, 2 dozen red peppers, 30 onions (medium size), 2 quarts vinegar, 3 cups sugar, 6 tablespoons salt. Put through food chopper; scald in hot water 5 minutes. Take vinegar, sugar, salt; let it come to a boil, add the above and boil 5 minutes.
— Mrs. Sodemann.

Pepper Relish

One dozen large, green tomatoes, 3 or 4 green peppers, 2 onions chopped fine, 1 tablespoon white mustard seed, 2 cups vinegar, ½ cup brown sugar. Cook all together until soft. Salt to taste.
— Mrs. C. H. Massow.

Relish

One peck green tomatoes, 1 dozen large onions, 1 solid head of cabbage, 1 large bunch of celery, 1 dozen green peppers, 5 cents celery seed, two 10-cent cans Coleman's mustard, 1 gallon cider vinegar, 1 pound flour, 1½ pounds brown sugar. Chop coarse; make paste of sugar, mustard, flour and add to boiling vinegar. Drop all ingredients into vinegar paste and boil a short time. Use turmeric coloring.
— Mrs. Graser.

Tomato Relish

Four medium size apples, 24 ripe tomatoes, 8 medium size onions, 6 green peppers, 3 stalks celery, 2½ tablespoons salt, 1 cup vinegar, 1 cup brown sugar. This makes 6 pints. Boil about 2 hours.
— Flora Hemler.

Cold Tomato Relish

Scald and skin 1 peck of ripe tomatoes. Dice them or put them through the meat grinder. Add 1 cup salt, and let them stand all night. Drain thoroughly. Add 2 cups of chopped onions, 6 red peppers (chopped fine), ½ cup mustard seed, 2 cups brown sugar, 1 teaspoon cinnamon, 1 teaspoon cloves, 1 quart of vinegar. Mix well and seal in jars.
— Mrs. G. Rausch.

Green Tomato Pickles — Sweet

One peck green tomatoes sliced, sprinkle with salt sparingly and let stand over night, 1 dozen good sized onions sliced rather coarse, 6 red peppers chopped coarse, 1 cup sugar, 1 tablespoon ground allspice, 1 tablespoon cinnamon, 1 tablespoon mustard, 1 teaspoon cloves, 3 pints good vinegar or enough to cover. Boil until tender.
— Mrs. G. H. Rausch.

Green Tomato Pickle

Four quarts green tomatoes, 8 large onions, 1 quart vinegar, 2 cups granulated sugar, 1 tablespoon salt, 1 tablespoon pepper, 1 tablespoon ground mustard, 2 teaspoons whole allspice, 2 teaspoons whole cloves, 1 teaspoon mace. Peel and slice onions, and slice but do not peel the tomatoes. Dissolve the sugar in the vinegar and pour the syrup over the tomatoes, onions and spices. Heat gradually and simmer until the vegetables are tender, stirring every now and then to prevent scorching.
— Mrs. Albrecht.

Chopped Green Tomato Pickle

One-half peck green tomatoes (chopped coarse), 5 or 10 cents onions, 4 green peppers and 1 red pepper (seeds removed). Then put 1 cup salt over all and let stand over night. In the morning squeeze through cloth. Put on to heat. Throw in 3 pints water and vinegar, half and half. Then squeeze through cloth again. Then put 3 pints more vinegar on to boil with some whole cloves and cinnamon in a bag, and 1¼ pounds brown sugar and 3 cents mustard seed. When this begins to boil add chopped pickles and 8 German celery roots peeled and chopped. Heat all through and put in jars. Celery root must be boiled in a little water after being peeled, then chopped. Also add water in which celery was boiled.
— Mrs. H. G. Thoms.

CANDIES

BUTTER SCOTCH CANDY

Five tablespoons molasses, 4 tablespoons sugar, 4 tablespoons water, 2 tablespoons butter; let boil until (when dropping a little in cold water it will be brittle). Put in a pinch of soda before taking off the stove, pour on buttered plates and when cool enough mark in squares.

CHOCOLATE CARAMELS
One cup grated chocolate, 1 cup milk, 1 cup sugar, 1 cup molasses, piece of butter size of an egg. Boil until it drops hard; pour in buttered dish and before it cools mark off in square blocks.

MAPLE CARAMELS

One pound of maple sugar melted in a cup of sweet milk, add 1 tablespoon butter; boil until when a little is dropped in cold water it will be almost brittle. Turn out on buttered plates, and when cool enough mark in squares.
-Hannah Albrecht.

CREAM CANDY

Two cups white sugar, 1 cup light brown sugar, ½ cup vinegar, ½ cup water; boil as you would molasses candy. A few minutes before taking it off the stove add 1 tablespoon baking powder. Flavor with vanilla. Cool and pull.
— Hannah Albrecht.

French Cream Candy

Take 2 pounds of confectioners' sugar, whites of 3 eggs well-beaten, 2 tablespoons milk. Mix all together with hands. Make small balls ; roll with hands. When still soft add a pecan, or walnut, candied cherry, stuff dates with same, roll an almond in same, let the rest lay an hour or more on paraffin paper, then dip in melted bitter chocolate.
— Mrs. Louise M. Lafrentz.

Dream Candy

Two cups granulated sugar, ½ cup Karo syrup, ½ cup boiling water, 1 cup English walnuts, whites of 2 eggs, beaten stiff, vanilla. Boil sugar, syrup and water until a little hardens in cold water. Add this slowly to the beaten whites, then add vanilla and nut meats and pour on a buttered dish. Cut in squares.
— Johanna Kretchmer.

Fig Candy

Boil until it colors ⅓ cup water, 1 cup sugar. Do not stir while boiling but just before taking from the stove stir in ¼ teaspoon cream of tartar. Dip the figs in this syrup and lay on buttered plates to dry.
— Hannah Albrecht.

Fudge

Two cups sugar, 1 cup milk, 2 tablespoons cocoa. Boil until it reaches the "soft ball" stage, then take from fire and add vanilla

and a heaping tablespoon of butter. Set pan into a pan of cold water and beat until it begins to snap. Pour into buttered tins and cut into squares.
— Mrs. H. A. Zorn.

Divinity Fudge

Two cups sugar, ¼ cup water, 2 egg whites, 1 teaspoon vanilla, ½ pound dates cut fine. Boil sugar and water until it begins to spin a thread. Pour slowly over the beaten whites of eggs, whipping until the mixture begins to harden. Add vanilla and dates. Spread on buttered tins and cut into squares when cold.
— Mrs. H. A. Zorn.

Marshmallow Fudge

One cup cream, 2 cups sugar, 2 squares bitter chocolate, pinch of salt. Boil until a little dropped in cold water forms a soft ball. Then set aside for 3 minutes on back of stove. Butter a platter and cut about a dozen marshmallows in small pieces to cover the bottom of the platter. Take fudge from stove, beat for several minutes and pour over marshmallows. When cool, cut into squares.
— Johanna Kretchmer.

Marshmallow Candy

Soak ¼ pound granulated gum arabic in ½ pint water until dissolved; this is best done by standing the covered bowl in a pan of hot water on the coolest part of the stove and stirring occasionally. Strain and put in a saucepan with ½ pound powdered sugar, set over hot water and stir over the fire until the mixture becomes thick and white; test by dropping a little into cold water; when it

forms a firm ball take from fire and stir it into the whites of 3 stiffly beaten eggs. Beat for three minutes ; flavor with vanilla or orange flower water and pour it into a pan which has been thickly dusted with cornstarch and of such size that the paste will be in a layer one inch thick. Stand in a cool, dry place over night, then turn out. Cut into squares, dust with confectioners' sugar or cornstarch.
— Hannah Albrecht.

Molasses Candy

Two cups molasses, 1 cup sugar, 1 tablespoon vinegar, a piece butter size of a walnut. Boil constantly for 20 minutes, stirring all the time. When cool enough, pull it quickly till it is white.
— Hannah Albrecht.

Peanut Candy

Two small bags of peanuts, about 10 cents worth, fresh roasted. Shell and chop fine in wooden bowl. Measure, then take exactly the same amount of granulated sugar. Melt without water and soon as it becomes liquid (not allowing it to cook), turn in the nuts. Stir a moment, then put on a dripping wet bread board, and roll with a wet rolling pin very thin.
— Mrs. R. Albrecht.

Taffy

Melt in a new pan 3 ounces butter, 1 pound moist sugar. Stir well over a slow fire; boil 15 minutes. Pour out on a buttered dish and mark in squares.
— Hannah Albrecht.

Sea Foam

Three cups light brown sugar, 1 cup water, 1 tablespoon vinegar. Let come to boil slowly, stir only until sugar is dissolved ; boil to the soft ball stage. Take off, and when it stops bubbling beat in 2 stiffly beaten egg whites and 1 teaspoon vanilla. Beat till it will hold its shape, then stir in quickly 1 cup finely chopped nuts. Drop in small pieces on oiled paper or pour into pan and cut in squares.
— Miss M. Schneider.

Sauerkraut Candy

Boil 2 cups brown sugar, ¾ cup sweet milk, butter size of walnut, till it forms a soft ball in water. Remove from fire, beat to a soft cream and add ½ pound coconut. Mix well. Drop by spoonfuls on buttered paper.
— Alicia K. Steinhoif.

MISCELLANEOUS

Worth Knowing

Stewed chicken without mashed potatoes, and pork without apple sauce lose half their zest.

Fried onions fairly cry aloud for a juicy beefsteak, and roast beef without potatoes, browned under the meat, never tastes quite the same.

Potatoes are an accommodating sort of vegetable. They are good with all meats.

With roast meats, sweet potatoes are appropriate, as are squash, tomatoes, asparagus and stewed onions.

Baked macaroni is a fitting accompaniment to a roast, so are Brussels sprouts and scalloped or creamed cauliflower.

Celery should never be omitted when serving poultry.

Turnips, carrots, parsnips and cabbage are generally eaten with boiled meats. White peas, beets, beans, corn and tomatoes are good with either boiled or roasted meats.

Squabs and all game have lettuce with French dressing served with them and lettuce must be eaten with Virginia ham.

MEASURING WITHOUT SCALES

The following table will be found convenient when you are without scales:

One fluid ounce contains two tablespoonfuls.

One dram, or sixty drops make a teaspoonful.

One rounded tablespoonful of granulated sugar or two of flour or powdered sugar, weigh one ounce.

One liquid gill equals four fluid ounces.

One fluid ounce (one-quarter gill) equals eight drams.

A piece of butter as large as a small egg weighs two ounces.

Nine large, or twelve small eggs weigh one pound without shells.

One level teacup of butter or granulated sugar weighs half a pound.

One quart sifted flour (well heaped) weighs one pound.

A common sized tumbler holds about one-half pint.

Four cups liquid equals one quart.

— C. M. R.

Table of Measures

16 saltspoons — 1 teaspoon.
3 teaspoons — 1 tablespoon,
16 tablespoons — 1 cup.

2 cups — 1 pint.
2 pints — 1 quart.
4 quarts — 1 gallon.

— Lydia Bohnsack.

Cake Hints

A good pinch of salt improves any cake.

Half water instead of all milk makes a lighter cake.

If your cake rises in a mountain in the middle the reason is your dough was too thick.

If it goes down in the middle your dough was too rich, too much sugar.

The cause of large holes in cake is too much baking powder.

A pan of water in the bottom of the oven keeps the bottom of cake from burning.

Uses of Vinegar

One-half teaspoonful of vinegar added to the cold water used to mix the dough of pie crust or (lemon juice if preferred) makes flaky pies.

A teaspoonful of vinegar added to the water in which beef is either boiled or roasted means more tender meat.

A teaspoon vinegar added to the water when cooking string beans makes them tender more rapidly.

Stains Removed

Iron rust, remove by applying salt and lemon juice to the dampened spots, place in the sun or near the fire ten minutes. Rinse thoroughly.

Mildew

Common soap application followed by one of starch rubbed in thoroughly. Lay in sun for several hours then wash.

Paint Stains

Turpentine takes out paint stains.

Ink Spots

An application of equal parts of citric acid (lemon) and cream of tartar melted, mix and rub gently over stains. Then wash.

GRASS STAINS

Rub alcohol on spots before washing. For tar or grease, rub on butter or lard, then wash in cold soap suds.

TO CLEAN BLACK LEATHER, FURNITURE OR AUTOMOBILE SEATS

Five cents benzine; five cents boiled linseed oil; three tablespoons of lamp black. Mix thoroughly and rub in well.
- Mrs. O. A. Kleppisch.

INDEX

A Toothsome Potato Dish........61
Adirondack Salad....................72
Almond Cake.........................175
Almond Cookies....................157
Almond Cookies - small........157
Almond Squares....................165
Almond Torte........................207
Alsation Salad.........................72
Angel Cake............................176
Angel Food Pudding...............90
Angel Parfait........................215
Angels on Horseback (oysters)...15
Anise Seed Cookies...............153
Apple - Ruby Salad.................72
Apple Coffee Cake................139
Apple Custard.........................91
Apple Dumplings - baked.......90
Apple Filling........................170
Apple Fritters.......................131
Apple Fritters 2.....................131
Apple Fruit Cake..................175
Apple Sauce Cake..................176
Apple Sauce Torte.................207
Apple Snow............................92
Apples - baked........................91
Apples - baked 2.....................92
Apples - Russian style.............91
Apples and Prunes - baked.....92
Apricot Jam..........................219
Apricot Prune Dessert.............93
Apricot Whip..........................92
Asparagus - creamed...............56
Asparagus and Tomato Salad...73
Asparagus Pudding.................55
Austrian Carrots.....................57
Baked Apple Dumplings........90
Baked Apples..........................91
Baked Apples 2.......................92
Baked Apples and Prunes.........92
Baked Beans - Boston.............45
Baked Beans with Ketchup...45
Baked Crackers & Cheese..119
Baked Cream Fish..................18
Baked Fish..............................18
Baked Fish with Tomatoes.....17
Baked Tomatoes.....................64
Baked Trout...........................20
Baked White Fish..................21
Baking Powder Biscuits........137
Banana Cream Pie................111
Banana Fritters.....................132
Banana Salad.........................73
Bavarian Cream Chocolate..105
Bavarian Cream - Maple.......105
Bean - Green Bean Soup..........9
Bean Celery Salad..................73
Beef - French Chopped..........31
Beef - Pot Roast.....................32
Beef Loaf...............................31
Beef Soup................................9
Beef Tenderloin & Mushroom Sauce.........................32
Beef Tongue - Sour................34
Beef Tongue with Vegetables..35
Beer Soup................................9
Beet Salad..............................74
Bird's Nest Toast...................121
Bitter Almond Cake.............175
Black Chocolate Cake..........201
Blackberry Jam....................219
Blätter Torte........................208
Blizt Torte............................208
Blizkuchen...........................177
Blueberry Shortcake............144
Boiled Icing for Cake...........169
Boiled Salad Dressing............70
Boiled Salad Dressing 2.........71
Boiled Salad Dressing 3.........71
Boston Baked Beans..............45
Boston Baked Chicken..........26
Boston Brown Bread...........138
Boston Filling......................171

Bran Bread...137	Cheese Sandwiches...120
Bread Crumb Cookies...153	Cheese Soufflé...120
Bread Crumb Pancakes...133	Cheese Straws...121
Bread Pudding...93	Cherry Cake...178
Bread Pudding - chocolate...94	Cherry Soup...10
Bread Torte...208	Cherry Soup 2...10
Bride's Cake...177	Cherry Torte...210
Brown Bread...138	Chicken - Boston baked...26
Brown Bread - Boston...138	Chicken - creamed...25
Brown Bread 2...138	Chicken - creamed on toast...25
Brown Cookies...154	Chicken a La King...28
Brown Sugar Pie...112	Chicken Loaf...26
Brownies...165	Chicken or Meat Pie...28
Burnt Caramel Cake...177	Chicken Salad...75
Butter Cookies...158	Chicken Salad - mock...76
Butter Cream Filling & Frosting 169	Chicken Salad 2...76
Butter Cream Icing & Filling...169	Chicken Salad 3...76
Butter Scotch Candy...239	Chicken Shortcake...28
Buttermilk Doughnuts...132	Chicken in Sauerkraut...27
Butterscotch Pie...111	Chicken - Turkish Style...27
Cabbage - Princess...56	Chili Con Carne...46
Cabbage - Red...56	Chili Con Carne 2...46
Cabbage - Red French Style...57	Chili Sauce...229
Cabbage - steamed and fried...56	Chili Sauce 2...229
Cabbage - stuffed...48	Chili Sauce 3...230
Cabbage - stuffed 2...57	Chili Sauce with Celery...230
Cabbage and Beet Salad...74	Chinese Cookies...154
Cabbage and Hotdogs - Sunday Evening Supper...48	Chipped Beef - creamed...46
	Chocolate Bavarian Cream...105
Cabbage Leaves - filled...49	Chocolate Bread Pudding...94
Cake - Plain...191	Chocolate Cake...200
Candied Sweet Potatoes...62	Chocolate Cake - black...201
Caramel Cup Custard...94	Chocolate Cake - egg-less...201
Caramel Filling...171	Chocolate Cake 2...200
Carrot Jam...219	Chocolate Caramels...239
Carrot Marmalade...220	Chocolate Cornstarch Pudding..95
Carrot Pudding...94	Chocolate Frosting...170
Carrots - Austrian style...57	Chocolate Frosting 2...200
Casey's Delight...52	Chocolate Pie...112
Cauliflower with Sausages...50	Chocolate Pudding...96
Celery Salad...75	Chop Suey...47
Celery Salad 2...75	Chop Suey 2...47
Cheese Balls...119	Christmas Cookies...161
Cheese Fluff...119	Cinnamon Buns...148

Cinnamon Rolls...........................139	Country Style Sausage............37
Cinnamon Stars - Zimsterne....163	Crab Meat a la Cardinal..........77
Cinnamon Torte.........................209	Crabs - Creole.............................16
Citron Cake.................................178	Cracker Dumplings..................126
Clam Soup - cream......................10	Cranberry Pie............................113
Cocoa Filling..............................171	Cranberry Sauce.........................23
Coconut Cake............................166	Cranberry Sauce - spiced..........24
Coconut Drops..........................166	Cream Candy............................239
Coconut Filling.........................171	Cream Candy - French.............240
Coconut Macaroons..................166	Cream Cornmeal Puffs............141
Coconut Pudding 95	Cream Dressing..........................68
Coconut Sandwich....................178	Cream Pie..................................113
Coconut Vanilla Loaf..............179	Cream Puffs..............................168
Codfish Balls...............................17	Cream Sauce...............................89
Coffee Cake................................139	Cream Sponge..........................106
Coffee Cake................................149	Creamed Chicken......................25
Coffee Cake................................179	Creamed Chicken on Toast......25
Coffee Cake - Apple..................139	Creamed Chipped Beef with Noodles...46
Cold Slaw Salad.........................74	
Combination Salad.....................77	Creole Crabs...............................16
Combination Salad 2..................77	Crumb Cake..............................140
Conversions...............................246	Cucumber Chowchow.............231
Cookies......................................155	Cucumbers - ripe canned.......230
Corn - canned............................225	Cup Cakes.................................166
Corn - canned 2.........................225	Custard Pie...............................113
Corn - Fried.................................58	Daisy Cake................................181
Corn - Luncheon Dish...............53	Date Bars..................................167
Corn - Sweet Pudding...............58	Date Cake.................................180
Corn Bread - delicious.............140	Date Cake - French..................181
Corn Chowder.............................11	Date Cake 2...............................180
Corn Custard Pie......................114	Date Salad..................................78
Corn Dumplings......................125	Date Tarts.................................167
Corn Fritters...............................58	Date Torte................................210
Corn Relish...............................231	Devil Cake................................202
Corn Relish 2............................232	Devil's Food Cake 202
Corn Relish 3............................232	Deviled Eggs............................122
Corn Soup....................................11	Dill Pickles...............................232
Cornmeal Pancakes.................133	Divinity Fudge........................241
Cornmeal Puffs - cream...........141	Donuts(Doughnuts).....132, 133
Cornstarch Cake.......................179	Doughnuts...............................132
Cornstarch Pudding..................95	Dream Candy..........................240
Cornstarch Sponge Cake........198	Duck and Rice............................29
Cottage Cheese Pie..................112	Ducklings, Indian Style............29
Cough Syrup - good................218	Dumplings-corn......................125

Dumplings - Never-fail	125	French Pastry Cake	203
Economy Cake	182	French Rolls	147
Egg Cutlets	121	French Torte	211
Egg Pancakes	134	Fried Corn	58
Egg Salad	78	Fried Fish with Stuffing	18
Egg Salad 2	78	Fruit Cake	182
Egg Salad & Salmon Mayonnaise	78	Fruit Cake - my Christmas	183
Eggplant	58	Fruit Cake - white	184
Eggplant - stuffed	59	Fruit Cake 2	183
Eggplant Pudding	59	Fruit Cake 3	183
Eggs - deviled	122	Fruit Cake 4	184
Eggs - escalloped	122	Fruit Cookies	161
Eggs - scrambled with tomato	124	Fruit Dessert	93
Eggs - stuffed	122	Fruit Mincemeat	115
Elderberry and Grape Jelly	223	Fruit Salad	79
English Plum Pudding	100	Fruit Salad 2	80
Escalloped Eggs	122	Fruit Salad 3	80
Escalloped Ham	39	Fruit Salad Dressing	68
Fairy Loaf Cake	188	Fruit Salad Dressing 2	68
Farina Dumplings	126	Fruit Salad Dressing 3	68
Farina Torte	210	Fruit Salad & Whipped Cream	80
Feather Cake	182	Fudge	240
Fig Candy	240	Fudge Cake	202
Fig Pudding	96	Gelatine Pudding	106
Filbert Cookies	158	German Napfkuchen	150
Filled Cookies	154	German Sauerbraten	33
Filled Fig Cookies	155	Ginger Cake	184
Filled Noodles	128	Gingerbread	141
Filled Noodles 2	128	Gingerbread 2	141
Fish - baked	18	Gluehwein	217
Fish - baked and creamed	18	Gold Cake	185
Fish - baked white	21	Golden Salad	79
Fish - baked with tomatoes	17	Goulash - veal	50
Fish - Boiled with Green Sauce	19	Graham Bread	142
Fish - fried with stuffing	18	Graham Bread 2	145
Fish - Halibut with Sauce	19	Graham Cracker Cake	185
Fish Salad	79	Graham Cracker Cake 2	185
Five Minute Pudding	96	Graham Nut Bread	142
Flank Steak	32	Graham Torte	211
Flaxseed Lemonade	218	Grape Juice	223
Form Cake or Kugelhupf	149	Grape Nectar	217
French Chopped Beef	31	Grape-Nuts Fruit Pudding	106
French Cream Cake	180	Grape-Nuts Loaf Cake	188
French Dressing	68	Green Pea Soup	12

Green Peas with Bacon	63	Kugelhupf 2	149
Grits	36	Layer Cake	187
Half Pound Cake	193	Leather Cleaning	248
Halibut with Sauce	19	Lebkuchen Christmas cookies	162
Ham - baked and spiced	39	Lemon Cream	97
Ham - escalloped	39	Lemon Cream Pie	114
Ham - scalloped	49	Lemon Filling	172
Ham - scalloped with vegetables	49	Lemon Ice	216
Hanoverian Salad	81	Lemon Pudding	97
Hard Sauce	89	Lemon Pudding 2	97
Hard Sauce 2	89	Lemon Sherbert	216
Hasenpfeffer	30	Lemon Sponge	107
Hasenpfeffer 2	30	Lettuce Salad	83
Hash - baked	51	Lettuce Salad & Cream Dressing	83
Hazelnut Torte	211	Liver Dumplings	126
Head Cheese	35	Lizzie's Hermits	159
Heavenly Jam	220	Loaf Cake	187
Hermit Cookies - Lizzie's	159	Loaf Cake - imported	188
Herring Salad	81	Loaf Sponge Cake	197
Herring Salad 2	82	Lobster Salad	83
Herring Salad Appetizer	81	Luncheon Corn Dish	53
Hickory Nut Cake	190	Macaroni - creamed	60
Himmel's Torte	212	Mahogany Cake	203
Honey Drop Cookies	155	Maple Bavarian Cream	105
Horseradish Sauce	24	Maple Caramels	239
Hot Lemonade Torte	212	Maple Extract Pie	115
Hot Sweetbreads	53	Maple Icing	170
Ice Cream	215	Maple Nut Cake	190
Ice Cream - mock	107	Mapleine Pie	115
Ice Cream - vanilla	215	Marble Cake	189
Ice Cream Cake	186	Marble Cake - inexpensive	189
Ice Cream Cake 2	203	Marchionesse Pudding	107
Irish Stew	52	Marshmallow Candy	241
Italian Salad	82	Marshmallow Fudge	241
Jam Cake	186	Mayonnaise Dressing	67
Jelly Roll - delicious	187	Measurement Conversions	246
Kidney - Sautéed	54	Measuring without Scales	245
Kidney Bean Salad	82	Meat Dumplings for Soup	127
Kidney Bean Salad 2	83	Meat Loaf	37
Kisselsteine	158	Meat or Chicken Pie	28
Kisses	167	Meatballs	38
Kisses 2	168	Meatballs in Tomato Sauce	37
Krumble Torte	212	Meatless Loaf	66
Kugelhupf	142	Milk Soup	12

Mincemeat...................115	Orange Pudding...................98
Mincemeat - Fruit.............115	Orange Pudding 2................98
Mincemeat 2....................116	Orange Shortcake Sauce........144
Miscellaneous.................244	Oyster Cocktail...................15
Mocha Filling..................172	Oysters - Angels on Horseback...15
Mock Chicken Salad............76	Oysters - Escalloped..............16
Mock Ice Cream................107	Oysters in Grapefruit Shells.....16
Mock Plum Pudding...........109	Pancakes................133, 134, 135
Mock Turkey.....................41	Paradise Jelly....................223
Mock Turkey 2...................41	Parker House Rolls..............147
Mock Whipped Cream........104	Pastry Flour.....................205
Molasses Candy.................242	Peach Salad......................84
Mother's Surprise................98	Peaches Melba...................98
Mushroom Soup................12	Peanut Candy...................242
Mustard Pickles.................233	Peanut Cookies.................159
Mustard Pickles - sweet........234	Peanut Dressing.................23
Mustard Pickles.................231	Pear Conserve...................221
Mustard Pickles 2...............233	Peas - Green with Bacon........63
Mutton - boiled with oysters.....36	Pepper Nuts - Pfeffernüsse......162
My Own Plum Pudding.......100	Pepper Nuts - Pfeffernüsse 2....162
Napkuchen - German.........150	Pepper Nuts - Pfeffernüsse 3....163
Never-Fail Dumplings..........125	Pepper Nuts - Pfeffernüsse.....163
Non Pareil Salad Dressing.........70	Pepper Relish...................236
Noodles - filled.................128	Pepper Relish 2.................236
Nut Bread.......................143	Pepper Salad.....................84
Nut Bread.......................146	Peppers - Green Stuffed.........63
Nut Bread - wholewheat.........143	Peppers - stuffed a la Josephine...54
Nut Bread 2....................143	Peppers - stuffed.................62
Nut Cake.......................189	Perfection Salad..................84
Nut Cake - hickory..............190	Perfection Salad 2................85
Nut Cake - Whipped Cream...191	Picalilli..........................235
Nut Drops......................158	Picalilli 2.......................235
Nut Filling.....................172	Pickled Cherries - canned........226
Nut Wafers.....................159	Pickled Peaches - canned........227
Oatmeal Cookies................160	Pickles - olive oil................234
Oatmeal Cookies 2..............161	Pickles - Saratoga................234
Olinda's Sunshine Cake........198	Pickles - sliced..................235
Oma Kuehl's Tea Cake.........140	Pie Crust........................111
Omelet with Chicken Livers....123	Pineapple and Strawberry Jam.221
Omelet with Fried Tomatoes...123	Pineapple Dessert................99
One Egg Cake - plain..........192	Pineapple Filling................172
One Pan Pork Chop Dinner......50	Pineapple Float..................99
Orange Cake....................191	Pineapple Ice...................216
Orange Marmalade..............220	Pineapple Milk Sherbert........216

Pineapple Pudding............108	Prince Albert Cake............195
Pineapple Pudding 2..........108	Princess Cabbage...............56
Pineapple Salad..................85	Proper Time to Can 224
Pineapple Snow Pudding...108	Prune Cake.......................195
Pineapple Whip...................99	Prune Pudding....................99
Plain Cake........................191	Prune Salad........................85
Plain Cookies...................156	Prune Torte......................213
Plum Conserve.................221	Prune Whip......................100
Plum Pudding - English.....100	Pudding Savory...................24
Plum Pudding - mock.......109	Pumpkin Pie....................116
Plum Pudding - My Own...100	Pumpkin Pie - mock..........117
Plum Pudding - Thanksgiving..101	Pumpkin Pie 2..................117
Pop-Overs.......................144	Punch..............................217
Poppy Seed Torte..............213	Quaker Oats Bread.............145
Pork - boiled with cabbage.....40	Quick Potatoes....................61
Pork - stewed with vegetables..51	Rabbit - Hasenpfeffer...........30
Pork and Navy Beans..........40	Rabbit - roasted...................29
Pork Cake........................192	Rabbit - steamed..................30
Pork Cake 2.....................193	Raisin Bread or Stollen.......151
Pork Chop Dinner - one pan....50	Raisin Cake......................198
Pork Chops - breaded..........40	Raisin Pie........................118
Pork Tenderloin Larded......40	Raisin Pudding.................101
Pot Roast with Carrots.........32	Raspberry Delight.............109
Potato Balls.......................60	Raspberry Jam..................221
Potato Cake.....................204	Red Cabbage......................56
Potato Cake 2..................204	Red Cabbage - French Style....57
Potato Cake 3..................205	Relish..............................236
Potato Dish - Toothsome.....61	Rhubarb - canned spiced....226
Potato Doughnuts.............133	Rhubarb Conserve.............222
Potato Dumplings.............127	Rhubarb Marmalade..........222
Potato Dumplings 2...........127	Rhubarb Pie.....................118
Potato Flour Sponge Cake...198	Rhubard - canned..............225
Potato Loaf & Bacon and Peas..48	Ribs - filled spare................42
Potato Noodles.................129	Rice and Cheese..................64
Potato Pancakes................134	Rice Cream Pudding..........109
Potato Puff........................60	Rice Pudding - Delicate.....101
Potato Soup.......................13	Roast Rabbit......................29
Potato Soup - cream............13	Rock Cookies...................160
Potato Torte....................213	Ruby Apple Salad................72
Potatoes - Quick.................61	Russian Apples...................91
Pound Cake.....................193	Russian Rock Cookies........160
Pound Cake - half.............193	Russian Salad Dressing........68
Pound Cake 2..................194	Rye Bread Torte................209
Pound Cake or Almond Loaf..193	Salad Dressing....................68

Salad Dressing	70
Salad Dressing	71
Salad Dressing - boiled	70
Salad Dressing - boiled 2	71
Salad Dressing - boiled 3	71
Salmon - boiled	20
Salmon Balls	20
Salmon Loaf	20
Salmon Salad	86
Salmon Salad 2	86
Sand Torte	214
Sand Torte 2	214
Sandwich Filling	121
Sauce for Orange Shortcake	144
Sauerbraten - German	33
Sauerkraut	38
Sauerkraut	227
Sauerkraut Candy	243
Sausage - country style	37
Sausage in Potato Boxes	52
Sautéed Kidney	54
Savory Pudding	24
Scalloped Ham	49
Scalloped Ham with Vegetables	49
Schaum Torte	214
Scrambled Eggs with Tomato	124
Scripture Cake	199
Sea Foam	243
Senf Gherkins (Mustard Pickles)	231
Shortcake - Blueberry	144
Shrimp - creamed & peas	17
Snow Ball Doughnuts	132
Snow Pudding	102
Snow Puff	102
Sour Beef Tongue	34
Sour Milk Cake	187
Southern Cake	195
Spaghetti - Spanish	51
Spanish Bun Cake	205
Spanish Cream	110
Spanish Dressing	68
Spanish Spaghetti	51
Spice Cake - delicate	195
Spice Cake - egg-less	196
Spice Cakes - small	168
Spiced Cranberry Sauce	24
Sponge Cake	196
Sponge Cake - cornstarch	198
Sponge Cake - Hot Water	197
Sponge Cake - Hot Water Prize	197
Sponge Cake - loaf	197
Sponge Cake - Potato Flour	198
Sponge Cake 2	196
Springerlies	163
Squash Pie	117
Stains	247, 248
Steak - Baked Swiss	34
Steak - flank	32
Steak - Swiss	33
Steak - Swiss with Peas	34
Steamed Fried Cabbage	56
Steamed Rabbit	30
Stewed Pork with Vegetables	51
Stollen	150
Stollen 2	151
Strawberry and Rhubarb Sauce	103
Strawberry Ice	217
Strawberry Jam	222
Strawberry Pancakes	135
Strawberry Preserve	222
Strawberry Pudding	102
Strawberry Pudding 2	103
Strawberry Whip	170
Stuffed Cabbage	48
Stuffed Cabbage 2	57
Stuffed Eggplant	59
Stuffed Eggs	122
Stuffed Green Peppers	63
Stuffed Peppers	62
Stuffed Peppers a la Josephine	54
Stuffed Tomato Salad	87
Stuffed Tomatoes	65
Stuffing for Turkey or Goose	23
Suet Pudding	103
Sugar Cookies	156
Sugar Cookies 2	156
Sulze	35
Sunday Evening Supper	48

Sunday Night Salad..................88
Swedish Rye Bread......................146
Sweet Corn Pudding.....................58
Sweet Cream Cake......................180
Sweet Potato Pie..........................117
Sweet Potatoes - candied.............62
Sweet Potatoes with Cream............61
Sweetbread Princess....................38
Sweetbreads - Hot 53
Swiss Chard..................................64
Swiss Steak...................................33
Swiss Steak - baked......................34
Swiss Steak with Peas..................34
Table of Measures........................246
Taffy............................242
Tapioca Pudding..........................104
Tea Biscuits..................................148
Tea Muffins..................................142
Thanksgiving Plum Pudding...101
Thousand Island Dressing....67
Thousand Island Dressing2...........67
Tomato Ketchup..........................228
Tomato Ketchup - my own...........229
Tomato Ketchup 2........................228
Tomato Pickles - chopped green.....238
Tomato Pickles - green..................238
Tomato Pickles - sweet green........237
Tomato Relish..............................237
Tomato Relish - cold...................237
Tomato Salad - stuffed..................87
Tomato Soup - canned..................226
Tomato Soup - cream.....................13
Tomatoes - Filled...........................65
Tomatoes - Stuffed.........................65
Tomatoes - Baked..........................64
Tongue Salad.................................86
Trout - boiled with cream sauce.......21
Trout - Baked.................................20
Turkey - mock................................41
Turnip Cups with Peas.................63
Turnip Soup..................................14
Tutti Frutti 205
Tutti Frutti Filling.......................173
Twin Mountain Muffins.............143

Uses of Vinegar..........................247
Vanilla Coconut Loaf.................179
Vanilla Sauce................................89
Veal Breast....................................42
Veal Collops..................................44
Veal Croquettes.............................42
Veal Cutlets with Tomato Sauce........43
Veal Goulash.................................50
Veal Loaf......................................42
Veal Sandwich.............................43
Waffles..............................135
Waffles 2..........................135
Waldorf Salad................................87
Waldorf Salad 2.............................87
Waldorf Salad 3.............................87
Washington Cake........................199
Watermelon Cake........................199
Welsh Rarebit.............................120
Whipped Cream - Mock..............104
Whipped Cream Fruit Salad........80
Whipped Cream Nut Cake..........191
White Bread................................146
White Cookies.............................156
Whole Wheat Nut Bread..............143
Wine Cookies..............................157
Wine Sauce....................................90
Wine Soup....................................14
Zimsterne - cinnamon stars........163

Other restored and reprinted cookbooks from NYHR

The Modernized International Jewish Cook Book
by Florence Kreisler Greenbaum, 1919

German Cookery for the American Home
by Ella Oswald, 1910

The Art of German Cooking and Baking Recipes to Keep Your Heritage Alive
by Lina Meier, 1922

God Bless Potatoes: The Modernized Book of Potato Cookery
by Mrs. Mary L. Wade, 1918

Visit us on the web

www.NewCenturyGermanCooking.com

and join our "German Cooking" group on Facebook

www.ingramcontent.com/pod-product-compliance
Lightning Source LLC
Chambersburg PA
CBHW030137170426
43199CB00008B/105